Lawrence E. Thompson

Where on Earth Is God?

Where on Earth Is God?

by
Dick Howard

Beacon Hill Press of Kansas City
Kansas City, Missouri

Permission to quote from the following copyrighted versions is acknowledged with appreciation:

New American Standard Bible (NASB), © The Lockman Foundation, 1960,
1962, 1968, 1971, 1972, 1973, 1975, 1977.

New English Bible (NEB), © The Delegates of the Oxford University Press
and The Syndics of the Cambridge University Press, 1961, 1970.

The Holy Bible, New International Version (NIV), copyright © 1978 by the
New York International Bible Society.

New Testament in Modern English (Phillips), Revised Edition © J. B.
Phillips 1958, 1960, 1972. By permission of the Macmillan Publishing
Co., Inc.

Revised Standard Version of the Bible (RSV), copyrighted 1946, 1952, ©
1971, 1973.

Unless otherwise indicated all quotations are from the *New American Standard Bible.*

None of us have adequate answers. Questions about suffering have baffled the greatest minds of the ages. What we do have is a God who is worthy of our implicit trust, and this book will strengthen your faith in Him!

Contents

Foreword

It was a peaceful summer evening. I sat with the author of this book beside a lake in Maine where his family had invited mine for a week's vacation. It was an enchanted evening. The fleecy clouds in the west, which a few minutes before had been colored by the sunset in brilliant hues of red and orange, were now fading in the twilight. The surface of the water glimmered like crystal. The soothing silence was broken only by the occasional splash of a fish and the gentle lapping of the waves against the shoreline. We sat enthralled, beholding the heavens' handiwork; talking little, but communing as friend with friend on that higher level that transcends verbal conversation. We sat enraptured, at peace with nature and with nature's God. The pain and suffering of the world seemed millions of miles away.

But strangely enough, that is what we began to talk about, as the twilight turned to darkness and the stars came out—*the problem of human suffering.* I do not know why the subject came up in such an unlikely setting. Perhaps it is because the world's ugliness is never very far away from its beauty—to those who are called to serve. Perhaps it is because the two of us had suffered some together, and in a moment of fellowship in the midst of nature's loveliness we were reminded of other times when we had become bonded together in the "fellowship of suffering."

Of course, neither of us has suffered like so many do in today's world. We have had reasonable health and sufficient food, clothing, and shelter for ourselves and our families.

But we both have known a little of the anguish that comes to those who have counted the cost of discipleship and decided to pay it, the cost of taking up one's cross and following Jesus, and maintaining one's integrity in the midst of misunderstanding.

At any rate, it was there by the lakeside that Dick told me he wanted to write a book about suffering. I urged him to do so and even suggested the title which he has decided to use.

This is not a philosophical treatise on the age-old problem of natural evil, although in Part II the author deals with the main philosophical solutions that have been offered. But he deals with them in plain, practical words—"plain truth for plain people," as John Wesley would have put it. He writes not merely from his expertise as a biblical scholar. He draws profusely from his own rich experience, first as a pastor and later as a college professor, giving the actual life experiences of people who have suffered and to whom he has sought to minister.

This is a book for those who are hurting. It is a book for those who have ever asked, as our Lord asked in His last words upon the Cross, "My God, my God, *why* . . . ?" It is a book for those who have ever cried out in anguish or in anger, "Where on earth is God?"

It is not meant as a book on technical theology, but its theology is sound—far more sound than much that we hear from today's "miracle peddlers" (to use the author's own words). The concept of God that comes through these pages is truly the *Christian* God; and the concept of faith that is explicated here is *Christian* faith.

—ROB L. STAPLES
Professor of Theology
Nazarene Theological Seminary

Preface

Countless times, as a pastor and professor, I have heard expressed in many different ways a heartrending cry: "Where on earth is God?" Sometimes it was hopeless desperation, but other times a hurting soul was looking in vain for God—here on earth.

This is technically the "problem of evil," or suffering, and is soon met in philosophical and theological studies. From the perspective of morality it is without doubt the most difficult, and even agonizing, question with which man has ever wrestled. More than 35 years ago I struggled with it academically, while studying philosophy in graduate school. To me it became increasingly clear that there was no fully satisfactory rational solution. Could the reason be that it tends to become a "nonrational," or even an emotional, problem? Regardless, as I worked through it theoretically, I did find peace—rationally and spiritually.

Now, after seeing the "enfleshment" of suffering with all of its hurting, I have tried to suggest a place of help. Repeated illustrations are given, which came through personal encounter, often with a broken heart. How different than classroom theories.

I am convinced that many times our suffering is intensified by *a wrong conception of God.* From our limited perspective we expect from God what He has not promised. At times, as Hebrews makes clear (12:5-11), our suffering *is* at the hand of God! But then He has the clear purpose of disciplining His children. Furthermore, it is specifically suffering *for our faith*. To assume that all suffering is God's discipline is unwarranted and causes needless heartache.

It is true that some find peace in their faith that God lovingly plans all of life's hurts. Thus Joni concluded: "Today, as I look back, I am convinced that the whole ordeal of my paralysis was inspired by His love."[1] This is understandable, given her theological presupposition of the absolute sovereignty of God. Even Hannah Whitall Smith, from a totally different theological perspective, found it necessary to relate all of our suffering to God. She pictured God's encircling presence being pierced only by His permission. Denying that God was the *author* of evil, she insisted He must be its *agent*.[2] Unfortunately, the logical and practical implications of such views of suffering are seldom considered. As a result, many do not find help but know only frustration, despair, and bitterness.

My purpose has not been to theoretically examine the philosophical problem of evil. Instead, I have suggested a practical understanding of God's role in our suffering that can bring a new perspective and peace.

Appreciation is expressed to Bethany Nazarene College for the sabbatical leave that made this writing project possible. Dr. Rob Staples, a close friend and former colleague, suggested the title. A special word of thanks is given to Wini, my wife, who repeatedly read and critiqued the material.

Several years ago one of my closest ministerial friends suffered the tragic death of his twelve-year-old son Christian—better known as "Chip." The faith and courage of Rev. and Mrs. Karl Retter, since that automobile accident, have been a lasting inspiration to me. It is with deep gratitude that I dedicate this book to the memory of Chip, and to his mother and father, who know what it means to ask the question: "Where on earth is God?"

"Chippah"

You've joined my catalogue of questions, Chip!
   Answers?—the supply never matches the
      demand.
I'm that awkward child-youth who caught your
      pitches
   Before or after a playful romp piggy-back style.
Trying to impress—I was thwarted by an
      exuberance
   I found enviable; wanted to enjoy my stage of
      life
As much as you did yours. I deny the possibility
   Of your being gone: Curse unfairness—its
      inevitability.

Through the sadness, a feeling rises as if pushed
By memory combined with evolving hope.
You live in every person who *lives* life flushed
By the briskness of vitality. You help me cope
   With sluggish views, a life that oft seems gray;
   You'll live on, in the son I'm gonna have some
      day!

Roy Howard
February 14, 1970

A poem written by the author's son and sent to Chip's parents at the time
   of his death.

Introduction

Six-year-old Harvey prayed:
> Dear God: Charles my cat
> got run over, and if you made it happen
> you have to tell me why.[1]

How do we react when we hurt, or when we see others hurt? Do we ask, even demand, to know "why?" Do we wonder, or maybe even put into words: "Where on earth is God?" Is He here on earth? Could He be here and allow such hurting?

These questions have agonized the mind of man as long as he has lived, and we ask the same questions today. What are we to do with this problem of suffering or evil? It won't just go away! Are there any answers? What attitude should we take? Is there any alternative to either a blind faith or a bitter resentment?

We must be candid! It is sheer fantasy to imagine that we can find a totally satisfying *rational* answer to questions that have hounded and baffled the greatest minds of the ages. Yet there must be help, somewhere.

A good place to start is to recognize our limitations. This isn't easy for humans who like to think they can handle whatever life might bring. Any understanding we might come to is strictly from our human perspective. There is no way we can see things as God does.

When calamity left Job on the ash heap, he sought an answer. He knew that his "sorry comforters" (16:20) were wrong when they insisted that he must have sinned. He had faith in God, even though he looked for Him in vain (23:8-10). But it was not until God showed him how little he knew that Job finally "saw" God (42:5). Then he found peace, not in an explanation, but in the presence of God.

Yet all suffering is not physical or material. Paul agonized over the fate of his nation, Israel. He even expressed a willingness to be accursed, separated from Christ, if that would bring about their salvation (Rom. 9:2-3). A careful study of Romans 9—11 reveals that the apostle never did find satisfaction in some answers he projected, such as "the total sovereignty of God" or "the responsible freedom of man" or "God's plans for the destiny of the human race." Instead, he found peace just where we must.

> Oh, the depth of the riches both of the wisdom and knowledge of God! How unsearchable are His judgments and unfathomable His ways! ... For from Him and through Him and to Him are all things. To Him be the glory forever. Amen *(Rom. 11:33, 36)*.

Paul had learned, on the Damascus Road, that our question to God must be "what?" and not "why?" (Acts 22:1).

Ultimately this is the only way any of us will ever find peace. Few, if any, can ask God "why?" in a Christian manner. We end up demanding vindication and not seeking for an explanation. Instead, we must ask, "What do You want me to do?" or "What is there here for me to learn?" It is our basic faith in God's love that brings peace.

Yet, I have come to deeply believe that many of us needlessly intensify and compound our suffering because of mistaken ideas about God. We must seriously ask ourselves what God has promised to do for us as His children. I think of a poem that hung on our bedroom wall for many years. It was a loving wedding present from one of our first church members.

God hath not promised skies always blue,
Flower-strewn pathways all our lives through;
God hath not promised sun without rain,
Joy without sorrow, peace without pain.
But God hath promised strength for the day,
Rest for the labor, light for the way,
Grace for the trial, help from above,
Unfailing sympathy, undying love.
                    —ANNIE JOHNSON FLINT

Most of us know this and believe it. But as we face the unknown—perhaps an operation, a long trip, a new year, or even a new day—*what do we expect?* Do we have some vague idea of a protecting Providence or even a guardian angel? How do we pray? What do we ask?

Oh, everything is beautiful when nothing happens. The operation is a success. The trip is safely completed. Another year or day comes to a close with no trauma. We even thank God for His loving care.

But what if something does happen? How do we feel then—disappointed, depressed, crushed, bewildered? On a Sunday morning Mrs. James rose in church and gave praise to God for His providential care during a vacation trip of thousands of miles. She and her husband had even observed a fatal accident, but God had wonderfully protected them. Yet, in that service sat a grieving mother. In fact, it was the first time she had been able to come to church since her only son had been killed in a traffic accident that summer. Can you imagine the questions that flooded her mind? Where was God when George's car skidded on the wet pavement and crashed into an oncoming car, leaving five dead?

Are we right in tying suffering, or blessing, directly to God? Does He either plan it or specifically permit it? We were all shocked and outraged when three masked gunmen kidnapped 26 young schoolchildren and their bus driver. Then after 16 hours in a buried moving van, they managed to escape. There was little visible physical harm, but many of the psychological scars remain and may never be erased. We all agree that it was terrible and tragic, but was the conclusion of the bus driver, 10 months later, justified? He said: "I guess God had a purpose for this."[2] Did God have anything to do with it? Should we blame Him?

Yet, repeatedly, that is exactly what so many of us do. When calamity, suffering, serious illness, accident, tragic loss, etc., come, we instinctively place the blame on God. He is tied to everything that happens. What we really are asking is why He didn't stop it! Has He promised to?

Such things stagger the faith of the believer. How could God let it happen to me? The unbeliever is certain that this is evidence that there is no God, at least one who is all-powerful and loving. Rob Reiner, of "All in the Family" fame played the role of "Meathead," a professed atheist because he couldn't accept the evil and suffering in the world. Unfortunately, there are too many with that attitude in real life who aren't playing a role. This was the last hurdle for the hero of Billy Graham's film *Time to Run.* "How can I believe in God when so many suffer?" he asked.

Could we be wrong? Do we compound our suffering because of a wrong conception of God? Maybe God didn't have anything to do with it! Perhaps He is hurting as much as we are! What does such an idea do to your idea of God? That is what this book is all about.

PART I

I Am Hurting!

Dear Father:
    Only You know how many of us are hurting—and how badly we hurt. Even more, You understand why we hurt. As we think about these reasons, help us to open our hearts and feel the hurting of others. It is so easy, and human, to close our eyes and hope the hurting will go away. We want to protect ourselves. But we are all part of this hurting world and need each other—and You. We know You won't fail us.   *Amen.*

If we have enough courage to open our eyes, we *know* this world is filled with hurting people, all around us. This isn't pessimism or cynicism, but simple realism. Perhaps, at the moment, we are more fortunate than most and are enjoying a respite. But sooner or later *everyone* hurts, the young and the old (and all in between), the rich and poor, the good and bad, everyone. Many things cause us to hurt in many different ways. But why talk about it? Isn't it better to push it out of our minds as long as possible? Can't we handle it that way? Too often that is what happens and we suffer alone, and that only makes it worse. It will help us all to honestly look at the things that cause our hurting. It should make us more aware of the aching hearts around us. Also, it will hopefully start us on the path toward the healing of our own hearts.

1

The Lights
Have Gone Out!

"I hope you have an answer for this!" Although more than 20 years have passed, I can still feel the shock and sting of those words. Bobby, an active boy of eight, had been killed by a bakery truck on his way home from school. Now I was trying to comfort his grieving mother. Mrs. Stanley, a distraught neighbor, upon learning that I was a minister, had suggested with cruel cynicism that I should have an answer to this tragedy. I am sure she didn't mean to be unkind, but she was hurting. For the moment, her hurt had blinded her to the realization of how much her remark would pierce a mother's broken heart.

Does anyone ever have a satisfying answer to death? Facetiously we say that the only things certain in life are death and taxes. Yes, we know that we are all born to die. But when death comes, it is still a shock. The lights go out, and the loss seems irreparable. We have no human answer, and we hurt.

This is particularly so when death comes suddenly to someone young or in the prime years of life. We can't help but feel it is a tragic waste. We think: What could have been!

It might be a child or parent, perhaps a close relative or friend. One day they are very much alive and a vital part of our lives, and then the next day they are gone, forever. It seems like our world has fallen apart, and there is no way that life can be the same again. The lights have gone out and we hurt.

But it is no less true when we realize that "our days are numbered." Often we speak of a merciful death, meaning one that is sudden and without suffering. A loved one dies in his sleep, or is killed in an accident, or drops with a heart attack or stroke. Even as I was working on this material, Mrs. Moore was killed by a fall down a flight of stairs. This elderly lady, a former parishioner, left behind a loving husband. He surely must have known that neither of them had very much time left in this world. Yet, those of us who know him continue to see the deep hurt in his eyes. The tragic death was not merciful *to him!* After the immediate shock, when the loss is increasingly realized, the agony of separation continues for those who are left behind. The lights have gone out and we hurt.

Even when death comes after a lingering illness and the slow disintegration of the human body, is it not the same? Oh, yes, we think we can prepare ourselves for the inevitable. We can even assuringly say: "They will be better off." Yet, when the final end comes, we aren't prepared for what happens. It isn't as we thought it would be, even when it is a relief from months or years of loving care. The sense of loss is so often bitter and painful, and we miss the lost loved one more than we dreamed. Death is so final!

We usually think of death in "personal terms,"—very personal. But sometimes it comes in major disasters. Every day the news media report a plane or train crash, a terrible fire, tornadoes or hurricanes, earthquakes—or something grotesque like the freak hotel skywalk collapse in Kansas

City that left well over 100 dead. Anywhere from a few to scores or even thousands perish—every day! In addition, every hour there are at least hundreds somewhere dying in the agony of starvation. Added to that is the horrible carnage of war, big ones and little ones. It all seems so impersonal, unless of course one of our loved ones is involved. Yet *people,* flesh and blood humans, are dying. And death always leaves behind emptiness, loss, and a deep hurt.

But why rehearse these facts? We want to forget them, don't we? Our answer to death is to try to escape it as long as we can. We try to drive it from our consciousness. We try to act like it will never happen to us. But it will! Our circle will be invaded and then we will hurt.

We want to find a way to handle this hurting. We can't do it unless we are willing to look at it with honesty and courage. Can we find an answer that will help us in those difficult hours? The first thing to remember is that it is only human to sorrow in the presence of death. Somewhere in our consciousness we often have the idea that an expression of grief is a sign of weakness. We think we ought to be able to stoically accept death and immediately adjust to it. It helps us to remember that the greatest Man who ever lived wept before a grave—*just like we do.* When Mary and Martha were hurting, so was Jesus!

What is of greatest importance is our *attitude* in the presence of death. After the initial shock is passed and we begin to try to put our lives back together, what then? That is what we are going to look at, honestly and hard. At this point we simply want to accept the fact that for *everyone* death hurts. There are only some who show it more than others. But we all hurt!

2

The Shadows
Are Falling

I stood at my desk, stunned. Word had just reached me that Jim, one of my finest students, had leukemia. It seemed so unreal. Only the day before he had sat in my class, participating with his usual eager desire to learn. Now it would be all over in a few months or, at the most, in a year or two. What a loss! He was just getting started in his ministerial training. Every indicator pointed to a future bright with promise and possibly brilliance. It was easy to picture him as the devoted pastor of a growing congregation. Perhaps in time he might even have become an instructor of other ministerial students. But with shocking suddenness, the shadows were falling. Jim was hurting and my heart reached out to him.

The shadows fall in many different ways. Probably the most common cause is cancer. Thank God that medical science is pursuing this killer with an almost fanatical dedication. As a result, there is much more hope today than even 5 or 10 years ago. Yet the word *cancer* still sends a chilling shudder down our spines. I would guess that most of us, at least subconsciously, live with a fear of hearing those terrifying words: "You have cancer."

Not long ago I enjoyed being in Bill Thomas' church for a weekend of special services. He and I spent many hours together. He seemed to be in good health. The fellowship around the table at mealtime, in the parsonage, was a delight. We became good friends and shared many interests and concerns. Then, *less than a week after I was with him,* Bill discovered he had a form of cancer that is often fatal. He had operations and both chemical and radiation therapy. For a time, it even seemed like he was going to recover. But then, with savage suddenness, he took a turn for the worse and died. He left behind several children as well as his wife. One daughter was not yet of school age. Death was bad enough, but the heartache of anticipation as the shadows fell compounded the hurting manyfold.

Sometimes it is an inoperable tumor that will bring certain death. Other times it is a failing heart or a diseased liver or kidney. With the advent of organ transplants and more recently the development of plastic organs, such a person has a glimmering of hope. Yet, when the case histories are examined, these modern medical wonders seldom succeed in doing more than postponing the fatal day. At best the shadows fall a bit slower.

When death comes without warning, the victim seldom hurts, at least for very long. We have seen that it is the survivors who hurt. But when *we* are placed under the sentence of death, it is an entirely different matter. Here is a new and different dimension of hurting, in fact a double dimension. Both victims and survivors suffer.

It must be an experience totally unlike anything else we have experienced to *know* that our days are numbered—the shadows are falling. We all know that death is coming, sooner or later, but somehow we manage to keep our attention on the brighter fact of living. How can we ignore the bells when they begin to toll? Have you ever wondered how it would feel to know you are going to die—soon? Some years ago a midwest newspaper offered a sizeable prize to the person giving the best answer to the question: "What would you do if you had a million dollars and knew you had only one year to live?" A wide range of answers were received, indicating widely differing values. Some were very honorable and idealistic, while others reflected selfishness, greed, and even wild profligacy.

But it is one thing to hypothetically *think* about facing death, and an entirely different matter to be actually living under such a sentence. What do we do if we know that we only have a prescribed period of time to live? Without question this is determined, in great part, by our relationship with God and our understanding of Him. That is why we are thinking about these things. If, with Paul, we can say that "to live is Christ," then we should be able to go on and say with him that "to die is gain" (Phil. 1:21). But is it normal to want to die? Isn't it natural to love life and want to live? Is there something wrong with my faith in God if I don't want to die?

We need to learn how to handle this hurt. One of the saddest responsibilities I had as a pastor was to visit someone for whom the shadows were falling. Probably it was necessary for reasons I did not understand, but it always seemed heartless to have a section in a hospital or nursing home identified as the "terminal ward." Such people hurt in a very special way.

The shadows might not be falling for us, but we are unusual if someone close to us is not facing this circumstance. God does have help, and we need to find it so that we can share it with others.

3

Lost Treasure

Have you ever stopped to ask: "What is the greatest treasure that I possess?" What do you value above everything else and is the last thing in this world that you would want to lose? In fact, you could adjust more easily to the loss of anything, and if necessary everything, rather than this. I would think that it would be your health, especially if the loss were sudden. To *one day* be strong and apparently in good health, and then the *next day* to realize it was gone, perhaps forever, is certainly a lost treasure. You are no longer able to work, and your activities are curtailed, perhaps even to a wheelchair or a sick bed. Your greatest treasure is lost and you hurt.

Ruel was not only the lay leader of my church but also a close personal friend. We spent many happy hours together, hunting, fishing, and golfing. In these times he often shared, with an open heart, some of his deepest concerns. He and his lovely wife, Dorothy, often entertained Wini and me, and their warm hospitality was returned. We simply enjoyed being together. Then it happened! Without warning Ruel was smitten with a stroke that almost took his life. It left him seriously limited. He could walk and drive, but the former days of robust activity were gone. When together, we tried to act like nothing had happened, so we ignored the arm that dangled almost useless at his side. But it was never the same. We could never talk about it. I saw the deep hurt in his eyes. He had lost so much.

Every day uncounted thousands of us experience this hurt. We have lost our greatest treasure. Sometimes it is an unexpected heart attack. Thanks to the amazing accomplishments of modern medical science, the initial attack is often survived. But even with the marvels of open-heart surgery, we are many times left with serious limitations. Our diet is restricted and every activity must be carefully monitored. We must watch what we lift and be careful of steps. We must never run, and do everything at a proper pace. Of course, we are grateful to be alive! But the limitations under which we must live are a perpetual hurt.

It is easy to forget, but it was only two or three decades ago when the polio epidemic came every summer. For this reason I dreaded the summers! Never a year passed but children in my Sunday School were stricken. How well I remember the times, late at night, when I slipped to the side of Judi and Roy as they slept, and with fear gripping my throat, prayed that they might be spared a life of crippling limitation. But I felt so helpless. Then the glorious news—a vaccine had been discovered! How happy I was to have my daughter and son serve as "polio pioneers." But in my gratitude I remember the many thousands not so fortunate. Today they still bear the results of that crippling monster and constantly hurt.

For some, arthritis is an inconvenience that causes intermittent discomfort and occasional aches and pains. But for others it is a constant disabling and crippling hurt. One of the sweetest souls I ever was privileged to minister to was the almost helpless victim of rheumatoid arthritis. Her limbs were so grotesquely twisted she was unable to even feed herself as she lay on a bed of unimaginable pain. Fortunately, her sight and hearing were unimpaired, and she regularly listened to our radio broadcast. I met her through the loving concern of a visiting nurse who was a member of my church. To my amazement there was no resentment or bitterness about her condition, not even a complaint. In spite of her constant hurting, physically and mentally, she always had a cheerful smile and warm greeting. I soon learned the secret. With childlike faith she was living in the strength of God's peace. When I left her bedside, there was an ache in my heart, especially when I saw the hurt in the eyes of her ever attentive daughter.

Another crippler, especially among young adults, is popularly known as M.S. (multiple sclerosis). Suddenly and mercilessly it strikes, leaving heartache and hurt in its wake. I met Jane in a nursing home, where she shared a room with a parishioner. Her cheery smile captivated me, especially when I learned her story. Jane had been a busy R.N. with all the dreams an attractive young lady has. Then M.S. struck its cruel blow. Only able to painfully walk with the aid of two canes, she spent most of her waking time in a wheelchair. Knowing the medical history of the disease, she forced herself to keep mobile by making an agonizing weekly shopping trip on the bus. Now, over 30 years later, I cannot hear the dreaded name M.S. without thinking of Jane. The manner in which she "handled her hurt" will always be an inspiration to me.

Few things hurt more than the loss of sight or hearing, be it gradual or sudden. As he grew older, my father-in-law beautifully accepted his growing blindness due to glaucoma, but we all sensed his hurt. When he could no longer drive, and then had to be "guided" around obstacles in his pathway, his loss intensified. His sudden death by a fall, caused by his blindness, was in many ways a blessing. He was spared the agonizing hurt of total helplessness that so many of the blind aged experience. When blindness comes in childhood, youth, or even middle age, the remaining years of painful hurting seem harder to bear. How inspiring it is to see so many learn to cope with such a loss.

In addition to sickness, we many times lose our greatest treasure by a disabling accident. Every day the newspapers are crowded with reports of auto or train collisions, fires, industrial mishaps, violent storms, etc., that leave behind hurting people who face the rest of their lives with handicaps of every kind. Added to these are the multiplied thousands, or even millions, who today are the surviving casualties of war. For many, what is left to them is little more than a living death. They did not make the "supreme sacrifice," but instead lost their greatest treasure.

These are but a few of the ways that the greatest treasure in life, our health, is lost. What do we do when this happens? Most of us learn to live with it, sometimes triumphantly, but often with bitterness. How can we learn to "handle our hurts"? This is what we are searching for. What God has enabled some to do can certainly be our experience also.

4

No Greater Loss

I was never asked a harder question! Brother Williams, an elderly church member who was not long for this world, asked: "How can I enjoy heaven and know that my daughter is in hell?" With utter despair he added: "Pastor, I don't want to go to heaven!" Seeing my dismay, he opened his heart and a torrent of anguish, locked there for nearly a half century, gushed out. A daughter of his youth had wildly rebelled against God, the church, her parents, and even her friends. There followed a life of deep sin and wickedness. Then, with sickening suddenness, her waywardness ended in suicide, as a prostitute! Everything he had been taught now told him that his daughter was in hell. The loss was so great that his broken heart could not put together a heaven for himself and a hell for his beloved daughter. Oh, how deeply he was hurting!

When we speak of losing our children, we certainly do not mean the hurt that every parent feels when the child he has born and raised reaches the age of self-determination and begins a life of his own. In our more lucid moments we realize that this is an essential part of parenthood. God never intended that parents and *adults* remain together, only parents and children. Tragic indeed is the aftermath of overly possessive parenthood. So often a parent's unwillingness to let a child live his own life stems from the parent's insecurity or even immaturity. Yet, he objectifies this as the imagined need of a son or daughter. Lasting damage is experienced by both parent and child.

Of course, there are the more stoical among us who insist that they not only desire but even welcome the day when their offspring will take wings and fly from the nest. But in spite of their voiced idealism, their very insistence is a screen to hide the hurt in their heart. It is good to realize that severed apron strings *should* cause pain, but pain that is tempered by hopes and dreams. In fact, the loss we are speaking of is not even disappointment over the failure of our children to fulfill those dreams and hopes.

It is only human to have ambitions for our children and to make plans for them. What could be more right than to provide for their future education and careers? Yet those we have brought into this world are free persons, and we dare not, indeed we cannot, deny them that freedom. There naturally is disappointment if they choose another path than we might wish. But this must never be viewed as *our loss.* Instead, in a very real sense, it is *their gain,* even the priceless treasure of exercised freedom. Only God, not parents, has the inalienable right to be intrinsically involved in that freedom.

The real loss we are dealing with is the sad aftermath of rebellion. It is the heartache we know when, through sheer wilfulness and sometimes spite, opportunities and privileges are prostituted and a path is taken that will inevitably lead to dissipation and despair. Standing helplessly by, we know that the day will come, perhaps soon, when they will fully realize it for themselves. It is not a matter of a child refusing to do what we might wish; rather it is his insisting on denying himself what one day he will desperately desire. When a child's will to independence not only denies him his greatest opportunities, but alienates him from parents who dearly love him, this is the greatest loss! Sometimes this alienation is open, resulting in a wasted life, but more often it is subtly hidden within.

It helps to remember that God was the first hurting Parent.[1] Could this be why Luke 15 is one of the great classics of Scripture? Is it because so many of us can personally relate to it? This portrait of "lostness" spans centuries and cultures and speaks to us right where we are living and hurting. Not only the two sons, but also the sheep and coin *are pictures of us!* Some, like the sheep, are lost through thoughtless wandering; or even by carelessness, as the coin. Such are *found* by diligent and even desperate searching. But others are lost by rebellion, whether it be the open profligacy of the younger son or the simmering resentment of his elder brother. *But rebels aren't found by searching!* Instead, reunion only comes after heart-wrenching *waiting,* if ever. They must come home themselves!

The graphic sight of an anxious father, nightly gazing into the dusk as it settled on the homeward path, hoping to catch a glimpse of his wayward son, is something many parents understand. How much rather would we go, at any cost, into the far country! It really is much easier than waiting. But the wise parent knows that his *searching,* though done in love, will only drive his prodigal still further away.

This is why only God, and to some extent one who has experienced it, understands our heartbreaking loss when we become strangers to our own children. How can we handle such a loss? Is there help for our aching hearts? Certainly an understanding God knows how to help us! We want to learn how to recover from our loss that is so great.

33

5

Torn Apart

Broken ties *always* hurt, no matter what the relationship! Even today I can see the haunting look on Mabel's face. As her marriage was dissolving in divorce, she pled: "Please don't forget to pray for me." As this century draws to a close, we are experiencing an epidemic of divorce in America that is frightening. Repeated statistics reveal that a marriage doesn't have an even chance of survival. Now there is the unbelievable specter of a "no-fault" divorce. How can there be such a thing? In divorce there is *always* fault, and also pain and hurting. Sometimes we forget that divorce involves people—adults and children. God intends marriage to be for life; so when it ends in divorce, the only possible result is suffering. Although we wear masks and play games, life can never be the same. No one is ever left unmarked. Lives, young and old, are permanently scarred by resentments and hatred. Only God knows how many suicides can be traced to divorce, to say nothing of a lasting bitterness that is little more than a living death. Many struggle with loneliness, insecurity, and fear for the rest of their lives.

Those contemplating divorce should honestly face this reality. We are so influenced by the world of fantasy, romantically portrayed on the screen or printed page, that we accept the make-believe as the real thing. All we see is the mirage of exchanging an unpleasant relationship, many times magnified, for an ideal dream. After all, isn't that what is fantasized constantly as the "norm"? Our eyes are blinded to the pain and hurting that *always* follows divorce. This is true even when divorce seems to be the only escape from acute incompatibility or physical abuse. As marriages are torn apart by divorce, the aftermath can only be hurting people.

Another modern heartache is caused by alienation, either within a family or between families. How easy it is to forget that bitterness *hurts most the person who is bitter!* We imagine that our wounded ego will be salved by harboring ill will. But it doesn't work that way! When relatives refuse to speak to each other and resentment persists for years, if not for a lifetime, everyone loses. How sad it is to find, often after many years, that the supposed offense was over a trivial event long forgotten. Life is too short for precious relationships to be thus torn apart.

Have you ever lost a close friend? Most of us have through death, and we learn to adjust. But when friendship is torn apart through misunderstanding or conflict, the hurt goes on and on. In one church I pastored, Frank and Harold were unusually close friends. I looked at them more than once and thought of Jonathan and David. It was a relationship that was beautiful in contrast to the sordid ones we often see today. I returned in later years to find that friendship ruptured because of conflicting opinions about a third party. They didn't hate each other! There wasn't even ill will between them. When they met, polite greetings were exchanged. But they had been robbed of something precious and beautiful, and it could never be the same again. My heart continues to ache for my two friends, but theirs is the deepest hurt. I can relate to their hurting because, after many years, I still feel the wounds caused by lost friendships. Without doubt, the ones that hurt most are where confidences were broken and respect was lost.

In our day, with all the tabloid and celluloid caricatures of love, it is easy to be cynical about romance. But is there anything more beautiful and priceless than "true love," especially for the first time? To see total self-giving, almost with abandonment, is inspiring. How thrilling it is to have that love returned in kind. But to love is *always* to risk. When our love is spurned, or after being shared, when it is torn apart by misunderstanding or disillusionment, we suffer one of life's deepest hurts. Many a modern ballad romanticizes a "lost love" and makes it almost desirable. Yet, the one experiencing such a loss doesn't feel like singing! Instead, his heart is breaking. If that heart is young and tender, the break leaves scars that often last for a lifetime. In fact, for some it is veritably impossible to love again as they once did. Their hearts have been torn apart and don't ever fully mend again.

Behind the masks that so many of us wear there lies deep hurt over a treasured relationship that has been torn apart. Can we find healing for our hurt? Are we doomed to a life of "grin and bear it"? Does not God understand love and broken relationships? Is not this what John 3:16 is all about—"God so loved ... that He gave [up] His only begotten Son"? When He suffered in every way that we do (cf. Heb. 2:18), that surely included having His most precious relationship torn apart. Cannot such a God help us?

6

The Bottom
Has Dropped Out

I sat across the lunch table from a friend who was obviously in deep distress. With a look of utter despair and hopelessness Ed threw up his hands and said: "The bottom has dropped out!" He was hurting deeply because he had prided himself on being a successful businessman. From a tiny beginning he had built a prosperous company, by hard work and wise investments. His assets must have made him more than a millionaire. Furthermore, he had honored God in his prosperity, generously supporting his church and many other needy causes. Now he was in serious financial trouble. An unexpected shift in the economy had turned several investments, which had seemed sound, into potential disasters. Before he hardly knew it, he was struggling to escape bankruptcy. In vain he had exhausted every avenue that promised relief. Now, with his back against the wall, he was hurting.

In this modern age with all of its complexities, when we experience a serious financial loss, it *does* seem like the bottom has dropped out, and we hurt. How many there are who don't know what to do or where to turn. The media regularly report the cold statistics of thousands of small businesses that fail and fold. For most who are involved, it is the end of hopes and dreams, perhaps for a lifetime. They had planned and worked and saved, but now it is all gone. Few have the courage and will to try again.

Our highly competitive society increasingly takes its toll on jobs that once seemed secure. Many times, years are spent in developing a job skill, only to have automation or advanced technology make it obsolete. With little warning we find ourselves unneeded and unemployed. To be sure, efforts are being constantly made to provide opportunities for training in new skills, but the need is never met. To see a college-trained engineer driving a taxicab is only symptomatic of the problem. How many there are like this who hurt!

In addition there is the constant pressure of economic instability. Large corporations or entire industries suffer from a recession or foreign competition. The result is that thousands are left without work. In turn, this has its effect on every segment of the business community. As prices rise and tax bases shrink, public employees cannot be adequately paid, and many lose their jobs. It is frightening to see large cities totter on the brink of disaster. When government seeks to relieve the situation by subsidies and increased welfare aid, the only result can be mounting deficit spending and a postponement of the day of accounting. It all becomes a vicious circle, and those caught in its whirlpool hurt deeply. The truth is that ultimately we all are involved as our interdependence becomes increasingly apparent. No man is an island, nor can he live in isolation for very long. Whether we like it or not, we in a real sense *are* our brother's keeper, eventually.

Ofttimes the hurt begins with a *fear* of financial loss. Anyone who has the courage to honestly assess the modern economic climate must feel at least a tremor, if not a shock wave, of uncertainty. Unless we have a foundation of security, from somewhere, the inevitable result will be a corroding fear. It is serious enough to face the legitimate dangers of an economic crisis, but the hurt is compounded by selfishness and greed entering the picture. Competition for economic security many times brings out the worst in human nature.

One night, while I was preparing to retire, the telephone rang. Bill had to see me immediately! He was usually a model of confidence and self-assurance, but that night he could not hide his fear and frustration. In near despair Bill shared the fear that his immediate superior was maneuvering to place a relative into Bill's managerial position. He was approaching the "frightening 40s" and was convinced that any possible job change had to be made soon. I can still hear him ask: "Pastor, what should I do?" Bill was deeply hurting because he felt the bottom had dropped out of his job security.

For some, a forced retirement brings a similar hopelessness and sense of loss because work has been their whole life. When, because of age or ill health, we can no longer labor, life seems empty and meaningless. This is acutely so when we feel our performance is still satisfactory and essential. We feel like we are being "put out to pasture." As we grow older, few things cause us to hurt more than a sense of uselessness.

Critical financial losses are experienced in other ways, causing us to hurt. We can spend most of a lifetime building a modest nest egg, or even a sizeable fortune, with an eye to the future. Then it can be suddenly gone through some bad investments or an unexpected emergency, perhaps a long, expensive illness. It is not only the lost dollars, but our savings represent years of time and effort, and very often personal sacrifice. We are left with practically nothing and it hurts.

For others, everything has been invested in a home, maybe a "dream house." We work and plan little by little until one day it becomes a reality. Then it is lost overnight by fire or some other natural disaster. Now our dreams are in ashes or ruins. Seldom does insurance give us a recovery of the total loss. But even if it does, that only can rebuild wood, brick, and mortar. It was more than house, it was our home; and in its loss, part of us died. Few have the courage to start again. We just hurt!

Is it wrong to hurt over financial loss? Isn't life more than houses, lands, and bank accounts? Should we not "lay up" for ourselves "treasures in heaven, where neither moth nor rust destroys, and where thieves do not break in or steal"? (Matt. 6:20). Of course life must be more than "mammon"! But we *are* living in this world and such losses *do* hurt. How can we find peace? What is the answer when the bottom drops out for us?

7

There's No Release in Sight

Maybe it is because I have been a teacher, and very much interested in education, that a witty statement has stuck in my mind like a burr. "No one has completed his education until he has learned to live with an insoluble problem." Here is another reason why so many hurt today. Perhaps they have not completed their education; but as they must live 24 hours a day in a situation for which there is no solution, they hurt. As far as they can see, there is no release in sight. Their problem and hurt is always there!

Sometimes it is a physically crippling condition caused by disease or accident. My acquaintance with this kind of suffering came early. Some of my first memories of pastoring are the visits with Mrs. Johnson, who had been paralyzed in childbirth. Every time, with radiant face, she would ask me to sing her favorite hymn: "Count Your Blessings." She was still counting her blessings, although for more than 20 years she had been confined to a wheelchair or sick bed. Joni, a teenager who suddenly became a quadriplegic because of a diving accident, vividly relates in her books the anguish of daily facing a hopeless physical condition.

41

But the deep hurt of suffering isn't always physical in nature. It was in that same tiny first pastorate that I met Grammie Olsen, the mother of one of my church members. In spite of repeated invitations she never had attended our little church. After several calls and appeals that she at least come once, finally she shared with me the anguish that smothered her whole life. Looking back after many years, I can only be amazed that sheer love spanned a wide generation gap. I was a very young and inexperienced pastor, barely out of college; and she was an elderly grandmother without too many years left in this world. She had not been able to talk to anyone, even her own children, but that day she poured out of her heart the hurt that so long had been bottled up there. She could see nothing but hopelessness and despair. God seemed far away and unconcerned.

Many years before she had, in isolation, nursed an only son stricken with meningitis; and she saw him die a painful death, although he was certain that God would heal him. For several years she had cared for one daughter who was seriously deficient mentally. In spite of daily heartaches she would not consider placing her in an institution. Added to all of this was another daughter, who was sexually sick. With callous cruelty she had brought home to her mother three illegitimate babies. Grammie was so ashamed that she was embarrassed to even go to the store. I can never forget the look of anguish on her grief-stricken face as she looked at me and asked: "Now, Son, can you understand why I can't go to church?" She could see no release in sight from her prison of hurt and suffering.

What is harder to bear than the knowledge that your child might die at any moment? Gene and Linda, a young couple I married, have lived with such a nightmare of uncertainty for many years. A doctor at one of Boston's famous hospitals told them, "I am sorry, but some morning you will

likely find Jimmie [their newly born son] dead in his crib."
All the marvelous miracles of modern medical science and
technology had not been able to remedy the damaged heart
with which he had been born. Yet the dreaded day never
came! Jimmie has reached high school and beyond. But for
Gene and Linda, there has been no release in sight from the
constant hurt that has haunted their lives.

Millions of people hurt as they face distressing conditions every day over which they have no control. Poverty,
sickness, and discrimination abound. There are whole na-
tions suffering under political oppression. For such there is
no *human* hope in sight, and they struggle to survive. Life
for them is mere existence without meaning. It becomes a
matter of endurance. Can they bear it? They have hurt so
long they are numb!

To recognize these conditions is not to be pessimistic,
cynical, or morbid. It is simple realism. We are living in a
world where people hurt for a variety of reasons. As Thoreau
said: "The mass of men live lives of quiet desperation."[1] The
all-important question is: "What can I do about it?" For
many the only answer is resignation, despair, or even suicide. Isn't there a better way? There must be, and we are
seeking it.

8

They Hurt Too

A church leader, knowing of my writing project, told me: "When you write about hurting people, don't forget the pastors." Then I remembered some of the hurts I had experienced as a pastor and spiritual counselor. Many of us tend to forget that those trying to help others are themselves human. Should we be scandalized when we see or hear of a minister who has "fallen on dark days"? It is not surprising that there is a high rate of suicide among psychiatrists and that not uncommonly a marriage counselor ends up in divorce court.

All too often, as pastors, we have a false image. We must never let others see *our* needs. Because we are an example, we aren't supposed to have any problems. But preachers have their needs like anyone else. When we have physical, marital, family, or economic problems, we hurt. What we don't realize is that it actually helps those we seek to minister to when they realize that we hurt like they do.

In addition to the hurts of our own lives, if we would be effective pastors, we will experience the hurts of others. It is impossible to help others unless we are willing to open our hearts and share with them. There is no such thing as being totally objective or uninvolved. The questions of others become our questions and must be answered. When we add their hurts to our own, sometimes the load seems unbearable. It is one of the high-risk factors of being a pastor.

There are also the hurts peculiar to the pastoral ministry. We have no privacy or life of our own. In a sense we are on constant display. Perhaps it is changing some, but we were taught in seminary that being a minister was a 24-hour-a-day responsibility. This does not simply mean that we are always on call. Rather, it is the fact that *at no time are we not ministers.* In the other professions we can put on and take off our coat of service. But wherever we are and whatever we are doing, we are ministers. This is a special kind of pressure that, for many, is hard to bear.

Of course, for the minister, there is the constant pressure to produce results, which is more evident in some church circles than others. We want to succeed! So we are driven by self-discipline. Added to that is the pressure of pleasing our congregation. We live with the ever-present question: Are they satisfied with the progress of the church? Then there is always the pressure of measuring up to the expectations of the denominational leaders. Are we satisfactorily responding to the flow of motivational programs? It is no wonder that an alarming percentage of pastors crack under the pressure. Others, seeing the handwriting on the wall, escape to other occupations.

Misunderstanding is a part of life, and we need to accept it as such. Certainly pastors aren't exempt from it. As long as we live in this world and work with people, we are going to be misunderstood. Yet, by the very nature of our task, we ministers are unusually susceptible to it. Although we know that misunderstanding and criticism are some of our occupational hazards, it hurts if our hearts are at all sensitive. This is particularly so when criticism comes from those we have tried most to help. Ingratitude is always difficult to take, and it hurts.

There is another area of hurting in many pastors' lives, particularly if we are spiritually sensitive. Because we are working with people, we are faced with the constant temptation to cynicism. It is so easy to be cynical when those we deal with disappoint and fail us—members of our congregation, ministerial brethren, and even our leaders. Sadly, some pastors succumb and seem oblivious to the poisoning of their own souls. But others, seeing the potential spiritual disaster, struggle to resist cynicism. We can't *really* help those we can't love and respect! So we are often in soul agony and deeply hurt.

How do we, who seek to minister to others, find help for our own hurts? This we need to discover.

9

Clouds at Sunset

As we identify those who are hurting, we need to remember the ones who have entered the sunset of life. Oftentimes there are clouds at sunset. Although more than 30 years have passed, her radiant face is still clear in my mind. I met Mrs. McPherson at the close of a service in which I had preached. I was deeply impressed by her words: "Many speak of growing old gracefully, but I want to grow old usefully." I couldn't believe it when her pastor told me she was over 90! Once an active lay leader in the church, her strength was now seriously limited. But faithfully Mrs. McPherson came by the parsonage on Monday morning and took what needed to be mended. She felt that this would assist the busy pastor's wife, who had four children to care for.

When the sunset years come, there is, of course, the nostalgic realization that the end is not far away. No matter how full and satisfying life has been, there is a pang of hurt when we know that we don't have long to live. Does any *normal* person want to die? Although we try to keep this hurt hidden, it is there.

An acute temptation, when we reach advanced age, is to feel useless. That is why it is so important to grow old usefully. It is only a short step from feeling useless to expressions of self-pity, that "no one cares," or "I am neglected," etc. Regardless of whether or not it is true, and most often it isn't, there is constant hurt.

For many of us there is the growing fear that we will be a burden on those we love. This is the reason why there is often an unreasonable insistence on self-maintenance as long as possible. We are not trying to make it difficult for our families, but we can't face the hurt of being a burden on them.

One of the most traumatic crises of life is when we simply do not have the facilities to care for an aging loved one. Their physical or mental needs cannot be met in our home. We are filled with guilt because of visions of lonely old people sitting around listlessly in a rest home that seems like a prison without bars. It is most unfortunate that we have such a negative image of nursing or rest homes. There are, of course, some undesirable ones where the primary concern is making money. However, many others have attractive facilities where the personnel carry out their most difficult responsibilities with compassion and dedication.

Still, at its best, life in a rest home is lonely! After more than 15 years I still have the sad memory of the hopelessness I found in the homes I regularly visited as a pastor. Even with the TV, the hours agonizingly drag on like a freight train with no end in sight. When I saw their faces light up, I wished I could spend every day there, especially the long afternoons. Their forced inactivity places them out of joint with the frenzied busyness we call living.

Countless millions of these worn-out pilgrims hurt—constantly. Is there any solace for this hurt? We *must* seek and find an answer!

PART II

What's Going On?

Dear Father:
We have been looking at the way people hurt. It seems like just about everyone is hurting in some way. Many have locked their hurt deep in their hearts, but it is still there. It is so natural to ask, "Why?" But when we do, we find that it doesn't help us very much. Even if we could know "why," that wouldn't bring healing. Instead, help us to understand "What?" What should we do as we hurt? Where should we turn? How can we find help? We are going to look at some of the ways people are trying to handle their hurts. What is there here for us to learn? Do these "answers" really meet our needs? With an aching heart we are seeking to find a satisfying answer. We are confident that You will help us. Amen.

Everyone reacts to life's hurts! With some the reaction is a quiet desperation that is hidden behind the mask they wear. But with others there is a violent eruption that scatters a fallout of protest and bitterness that is often expressed: "Why me?" Are we simply the helpless victims of fate? Is God, if He exists, totally disinterested in what happens to us? How much is the devil to blame for our troubles? Does God stand helplessly by as we suffer, unable to help us? Should we accept adversity as the loving discipline of God? These are but a few of the questions that haunt so many of us when we hurt. We probably wouldn't put it into words, but from deep within us there is often the cry: "What's going on?"

Our reaction to life's hurts is directly related to what we think about God. It will help us to realize this relationship as we briefly look at the ways people attempt to handle adversity.

10

Grin and Bear It

"The gods were finally through with her!"[1] Tess had been the plaything of the gods, and when they tired of their sport, they got rid of her. That's the way Thomas Hardy handled the hurts of life. Man is the helpless toy of fate. What will be will be; everything is predetermined. All of the experiences of life, good or bad, pleasant or painful, are inevitable. There is nothing we can do to effect them. All there is left for us to do is to accept what happens. We can either grin and bear it, or curse the gods of fate who hold our destiny in their hands. Each day is faced with fear and resignation.

How many of us are *practical* fatalists? We don't stop to consider the *philosophical* implications. When some adversity occurs, we simply conclude: It is meant to be. What we are saying is that we can't do anything about it and did not have anything to do with it happening. We are *victims* of fate.

I suppose this attitude brings a measure of comfort to some people. But it can hardly produce hope and peace. Resignation is not contentment.

Is this the way it *really* is? Does this honestly face the *facts* as we know them? Of course there are *some* things for which we can't see any cause. It would seem they are the result of some kind of blind fate. But are there not *many* things for which a cause-and-effect relationship is plain to be seen?

Sometimes, *we* are the responsible cause. One night I pled with Jim Clark to curtail his unreasonable work load. When I suggested that he would kill himself if he didn't, I proved to be a prophet. Jim was dead within a year from a heart attack. This was not some mysterious fate. It didn't have to be! When we ignore a proper diet, fail to adequately exercise, and put ourselves under unreasonable physical demands or psychological tensions, we are *inviting* a heart attack. Fate has nothing to do with it!

We can see this same pattern in many cases of lost health or accident. If we drink and drive, any mishap that might result has an obvious cause. Many tragedies have been caused by carelessness or indifference to safety rules.

Unfortunately sometimes we are the victim of someone else's irresponsible action. One of my closest friends was travelling late at night and was struck head-on by another car on his side of the road. Ralph's near-fatal accident was caused by a drunken driver in the other car. Again, it was not a matter of fate.

Even in the birth of a deformed baby there is a cause for the tragedy. It is not because the "gods" determined it to be so. Nor is it because "it was meant to be." Modern medical science might not be able to tell us what is the immediate cause of the twisted genes. But can there be any doubt that such a cause exists somewhere? More times than we want to admit, the cause is apparent: syphilis, alcohol, nicotine, drugs, etc. That is not fate!

When we really think about it, fatalism doesn't give us an answer to life's hurts. It really is a convenient cop-out as we curse the gods of our rotten luck. But life is more than luck, and we must look further for help.

11

I Needed That!

Rachel was dying of cancer and her grieving husband did not want to tell her the truth of her condition. I was surprised when Dr. Jones, the attending physician, objected. Later he told me: "I have observed that when a patient knows he is dying, he often discovers a hidden source of inner strength. He is able to more courageously face his ordeal."

This is a modern form of Stoicism that is purely humanistic. The original philosophical system known as Stoicism, which existed some 300 years before Christ, viewed everything as the divine will. All of the experiences of life, pleasant or painful, were to be placidly accepted. The only defense against life's hurts was to not feel anything! If we allow ourselves to enjoy pleasant things, we will be hurt by the painful. So, we must discipline ourselves to accept stoically, without feeling, whatever comes into our lives. Today, with all of the emphasis on pleasure, Stoicism in its original form is seldom seen.

The modern counterpart finds in adversities an inspiration to heroic behavior. Life's hurts are not to be passively endured but allowed to become a prod to personal achievement. Many of history's greats, knowing nothing better, lived by this philosophy of life. When the 50th anniversary of Charles Lindbergh's historic solo flight across the Atlantic Ocean was celebrated, more than one biographer noted his stoical character. He met every adversity as a challenge to be overcome.

While such an outlook on life is in many ways commendable, it is purely humanistic and often agnostic. Only through struggle, and the eventual triumph that follows, can we become stronger and greater persons. Adversity develops our character like physical exercise develops our muscles. The trials and obstacles of life, although they hurt, bring out the best in us. Thus understood, suffering is good for us. We should take the attitude: I needed that!

There is value in developing a healthy mental outlook. It is an evidence of weakness and childish immaturity to complain and cry when we hurt. Too many have never grown up! All of us need to face life's adversities as a challenge and not as a calamity.

Yet, stoicism *alone* is sadly empty and futile. We can only play mental games for so long. If we have nothing else to cling to except the vain hope that our hurting is helping us, the day will come when we are no longer convinced. The remedy seems worse than the disease. It's not worth it. We can either shrivel up with bitterness and cynicism, or we can curse the gods and die.

All of us need Someone beyond ourselves. We are no match for life's hurts. So we look further for an answer.

12

The Devil Did It

Flip Wilson took advantage of a common attitude toward life with his humorous cop-out: "The devil made me do it." Most of us relate to this because we like to blame someone else for our failures. More significantly, behind this escapism is the tendency to blame the devil for all of life's adversities.

Unfortunately, as in so many other things, people often have an extreme concept of the devil. Some are convinced that he does not exist and is only a figment of the imagination of the superstitious. A more sophisticated view is that the idea of a personal devil entered the Judeo-Christian faith through contact with Persian Dualism during the Jewish captivity.

But it is clear that Jesus and Paul, to say nothing of other New Testament writers, believed in Satan. That is good reason for us to agree. A preacher, with little formal education, wisely and slyly observed that we seldom meet those who are travelling the same direction as we are.

On the other hand, some blame the devil for everything that goes wrong. They conclude that all adversity is intrinsically evil. The devil is the source of all evil, so he must be to blame. They don't want to blame God.

But it is a serious mistake to conclude that all adversity is evil! Most of us have lived long enough to see that a wonderful good has often come from adversity, if it is met in the proper way. Joseph reminded his brothers, after their dastardly deed, that "ye thought evil against me; but God meant it unto good" (Gen. 50:20, KJV). God turned their murderous designs into a means of survival for a whole nation.

It is surprising that in probably the Bible's clearest picture of sin and temptation, the devil is not mentioned:

> Let no one say when he is tempted, "I am being tempted by God"; for God cannot be tempted by evil, and He Himself does not tempt any one. But each one is tempted when he is carried away and enticed by his own lust. Then when lust has conceived, it gives birth to sin; and when sin is accomplished, it brings forth death *(Jas. 1:13-15)*.

We are only tempted when we respond to the attraction of sin. It is the devil's job to see that there is something to "carry us away." He is the tempter. But the devil is not *all* to blame.

Even in the dramatic picture of the devil's treatment of Job, in the Old Testament, we must not lose sight of the central message. This picturesque drama is a challenge to the current belief that the righteous prosper and only the evil suffer. In great adversity Job's faith in God was "patient," not unperturbed but persistent (Job 13:15). God finally revealed himself to His servant, and he found peace in the presence of his Lord. This was a revolutionary solution to the problem of suffering. Even Job's return to prosperity is anticlimactic to the truth of this ancient classic. The *only* answer to the problem of suffering is the presence of God. Job was *never* given a rational answer to what had happened to him!

When we blame the devil for our hurting, we are not considering some crucial questions. Does the devil out-maneuver God? Is God not able to defend us from Satan?

We can't find a satisfactory answer to life's adversities by blaming the devil. We must continue looking.

13

There Is No God

"Now do you understand why I don't want to go to church? I don't see how there can be a God." Grammie wasn't bitter or vindictive. Instead, she was simply giving voice to her total despair. I had made a friend of this lonely and hopeless lady, who was more than old enough to be my grandmother. The compounded tragedies in her life (cf. Chap. 7) had driven her to the place where she doubted the existence of God.

There are uncounted millions who can only conclude that there must not be a God, at least a personal and loving one. Into their lives have come all manner of hurts. They have been stricken with illness or accident. Their loved ones are suffering. Economic or physical calamity has fallen. They look around and see the suffering of war, starvation, or natural disasters. If there is a loving God, He surely would intervene and stop all this.

There have been those who would assume an absentee God. One answer of rationalism has been to retreat to a philosophical system called Deism. Yes, God created our world but then departed and left it to run its course. He is totally disinterested and not involved. But to the common man such a God is worse than no God at all. The ancient

Greeks had evil gods who murdered and lusted, and were jealous and vengeful. Isn't a God who doesn't care and indifferently ignores our hurts just as bad, if not worse? It is better to conclude that no God exists. We can endure our hurts more easily if we feel that we are alone, rather than knowing there is a God who doesn't care enough to help us. It is like preferring to be an orphan rather than to have parents who do not love us. It hurts less.

But is this the right basis upon which to form our concept of God? Does it not reflect our frustration rather than what we really believe? But often we are trying hardest to convince ourselves. Is it not actually another cop-out when we face things we can't handle? Saddest of all, we don't find any real help denying that God exists. We are left in our misery. So we continue to search for a better way.

14

God Is Helpless

A world-famous teacher, under whom I was privileged to study, couldn't handle a personal tragedy. His brilliant mind recognized that we are only deceiving ourselves when our frustrations cause us to deny that God exists. But he could not accept the fact that God was able to prevent human suffering and would not. So, he developed the doctrine of a limited or finite God. He concluded that God was unable to do anything about our hurts. God was helpless!

I suppose it is better to conclude that God is helpless than to think He doesn't care about a hurting world. Weakness is preferable to indifference! We find it easier to believe that God is helpless rather than heartless. There is something contradictory about a God who doesn't care. If He can't be both, then let Him be loving and not all-powerful.

Yet it is difficult to honestly believe that God is helpless. Perhaps this provides a more satisfactory *rational* answer than believing He does not exist. But does it make more *practical* sense? Are we any better off with a God who loves and cares but is helpless, than with no God at all? Misery loves company—but from God? It is true that the empathy of shared suffering, from friends and loved ones, means much to us. It is a great comfort to have someone, with tears

60

in his eyes, grasp our hand and say: "I understand what you are going through because I have been there myself." But does it bring us any peace to know that God loves and cares for us and yet can do nothing?

At the very heart of any concept of God is the assurance of His ability to help us. Is it not as self-contradictory to believe in a helpless God as it is to portray Him as heartless? Somehow God and weakness don't go together. Aren't we just as well off with no God at all?

The idea of a limited or helpless God is a futile attempt to find a *rational* answer for an *emotional* problem. We can't reconcile in our minds the fact of a hurting world with a loving and infinite God, so we try to create a compromise that proves to be an absurdity. A finite God is more man than God.

A limited God does not explain our hurting, let alone help us. We turn elsewhere for an answer.

15

What Have I Done?

"If that is the way God acts, then I want nothing to do with Him!" That was the climax of one of the saddest stories ever told me. When I heard it, I was inclined to agree with the statement! Death had taken Tom's young son, and a minister had come to call. With misguided concern the minister heartlessly told Tom that this tragedy was God's judgment on him for the way he was living. The clear implication was that it would never have happened if he had not been disobeying God. Tom reacted with bitterness and disclaimed any faith in such a God. Now, more than a quarter of a century later, although I had won his friendship, I was unable to lead him to a place of faith.

In our more lucid moments we know this view of God is horrible. He does not express His judgment by killing innocent children! Yet, when was the last time *you* asked, in thought or word, "What did I do to deserve this?" Almost instinctively we view our suffering and hurting as a form of God's punishment.

When we realize that we aren't the unlucky child of fate and that life's hurts must involve more than some impersonal prod to noble achievement, when we can no longer blame it on the devil, when we can't conclude that God does not exist or is heartless or helpless, *then* we often feel that God *must* be punishing us.

We all know that oftentimes our greatest hurts come from the suffering of our loved ones. Gangsters and tyrants have for a long time used the threat of harm to those we love as a leverage for their devilish designs. But God isn't a gangster or tyrant! We can ignore the suggestion that He would punish us by hurting others. But what about God punishing us by inflicting us personally? What about a heart attack, a tragic accident, or economic loss? Could it be God trying to wake us up spiritually? It is very possible that such an adversity might *result* in a spiritual transformation. There are many testimonials to this happening. But that does not mean that God is punishing us.

This basic idea is based on the premise that we get what we deserve. When we prosper, we deserve it. When we suffer, we deserve it. An honest glance at life shows how wrong this is. Most of us would have a mighty rough time if we got what we deserved! The fact is that if there were any correlation between what we do (and are) with what happens in our lives, it is the opposite of just deserts. Most often it appears to be the best people who suffer hurts, and the rascals who seem to be blessed. There is no observable relationship between a good or bad life and adversity.

Of course the way we live does bring inevitable consequences. "Do not be deceived, God is not mocked; for whatever a man sows, this he will also reap" (Gal. 6:7). This is true of good consequences as well as bad. In fact Paul, in the context, is encouraging the Galatians to not lose heart in doing good. But Judgment Day is not on earth. God does not always pay off on Friday or the first of the month. The balancing of the books does not fully take place in this life.

It is a mistake to view *either* prosperity or adversity as a sign of God's evaluation of our lives.

It does not help us to conclude that our hurts are the result of God's punishment. To so view them is to unnecessarily aggravate our hurting *or* give a false sense of security to those more fortunate. There must be another answer to our quest.

16

It Is Good for Me

"I am trying so hard to accept it, but I can't understand how God's *making* me blind will be for my good and His glory." I had just finished preaching on Rom. 8:28, confidently proclaiming that God would make everything fit a pattern for our good if we would only trust Him. Now Mrs. Jenkins, a lady in middle life, facing imminent total blindness, stood before me as a flesh-and-blood challenge to that promise of God. For days her face haunted me. Was I guilty of glibly preaching a false hope? Then I began to understand a crucial distinction that is too often missed.

So many times we look at life's hurts as the *means* of God disciplining us. He has a purpose in what happens to us. Life's adversities are *designed* to mold or shape us into the pattern God has planned for us. One has expressed it this way:

> I'm a person God is making,
> Like a statue God is shaping.
> God is changing me, correcting;
> God's intent on my perfecting.

All of the disciplining is motivated by God's love. But the design of the purpose and plan is hidden from us. All we can see are the tangled threads of the *underside* of the

Weaver's handiwork. The beautiful design on the *upper side* is hidden from our view.

Even though we cannot see what is happening, we must learn to live in faith. We are to bear our hurts in joy as we trust the God who loves us and is working in us for our good and His glory. In recent years there has been an emphasis, among some evangelicals, that adds a further dimension to this attitude toward life's hurts. Based primarily on three Scripture passages,[1] we are told that *if* we are able to thank God *for* literally everything that happens, even the most painful and shattering experiences, He will transform even apparent evils into great spiritual blessings. What is too often forgotten is that this can be a subtle form of trying to gain righteousness by *our* good works. It is *our ability* to give thanks that releases God's miraculous power. A more careful study of these passages will reveal that Paul is urging his converts to *thank God for God* and not for the tragic ills that they are experiencing. They are to be thankful that they have God to turn to in times of trouble. This *spirit of thanksgiving* brings the peace that garrisons the heart and mind.

We all know, or should, that the most dangerous error is the one that lies closest to the truth. *God does discipline us!* The writer to the Hebrews tied together several Old Testament passages:

> And you have forgotten the exhortation which is addressed to you as sons, "MY SON, DO NOT REGARD LIGHTLY THE DISCIPLINE OF THE LORD, NOR FAINT WHEN YOU ARE REPROVED BY HIM; FOR THOSE WHOM THE LORD LOVES HE DISCIPLINES, AND HE SCOURGES EVERY SON WHOM HE RECEIVES." It is for discipline that you endure; God deals with you as with sons; for what son is there whom his father does not discipline? But if you are without discipline, of which all have become partakers, then you are illegitimate children and not sons *(Heb. 12:5-8)*.

This is a bitter pill for our modern undisciplined generation to swallow. *Sometimes* this discipline is *through* adversity. That is the immediate context of the Hebrews passage. But they were suffering *for their faith.* In addition, often the purpose of God's discipline is hidden from our view.

But does this mean that we are to view *all* of our suffering as the loving discipline of God? Only the most extreme individuals, who probably have never experienced intense suffering themselves, would suggest that we should. *There is a line of distinction somewhere, and that is precisely the problem.* We don't like to think, let alone talk, about it. It is better to drive it from our minds. A close pastor friend, whose young son was killed by a careless driver, confided in me that he could not handle his hurt. His only help was to refuse to think about it!

But if we are honest *with ourselves,* we must face it! Sometimes there is no redemptive element that we can see in our suffering, and we can't reconcile it with disciplining love. One of the first persons I called on as a young pastor was Mrs. Brown, an elderly lady dying of cancer. I have never forgotten, or understood, the long month that I called. Every day that I came I was certain that it would be the last. In another church I called for many months on a dear lady unable to move enough to feed herself. A pastor friend lives today with the aching knowledge that his first grandchild was born with an inoperable tumor behind her eyes. She is doomed to a life of blindness and probably much more. Such stories could be recounted by millions of people.

What can we say? Is such suffering the will of God? Does God *will* it? Are we to accept, in faith, such tragedies as the hidden, yet loving, discipline of God? If we see our hurting as God's discipline, what else can we conclude?

Many turn away from such experiences—broken! Some, who refuse to deny God, are doomed to a life of despairing resignation. Others curse such a God and *exist* in bitter resentment or commit suicide.

There is a modification of this conclusion, that suffering is God's discipline, which appears to bring some people a measure of peace. What does it have to say to us?

17

Permitted, Not Planned

Earnestly the young preacher explained: "God permitted it but did not cause or plan it!" He had just described a heart-breaking tragedy in which there could be no possible redemptive element. Unquestionably it must be evil, and a God who is good cannot cause evil. Therefore God permitted it, although He did not purpose or plan it.

Much has been written in theology books about the "permissive will of God." There are rational and theoretical distinctions that provide some "answers" for the mind, but they do not bring solace to an aching heart. We must be very sure we understand what we mean when we speak of God permitting suffering.

To some, the "permissive will of God" indicates a *general* or universal decision by God not to intervene in the tragedies of life. In this sense He permits or allows them to happen. To those who believe that is what is meant by the expression, we will have much more to say about the matter later.

However, to most people, the "permissive will of God" relates to a *specific* decision or choice by God to allow an event to happen. He does not plan or design it, but neither does He stop it. In fact, He does not purpose it and really does not desire it. Such an idea of God produces many problems.

Most obvious is the question of whether there is any *practical* difference between God not planning an event, and making a choice to permit it. Is not the basic issue His *personal* involvement? Is not God's will God's will, period? If my 10-year-old daughter were raped and murdered, does it offer any comfort to know that God did not purpose the tragedy but chose to permit it? Here is the heart of the problem of suffering when we view all hurting as God's discipline.

There are many troublesome questions that arise when we attempt to distinguish between God's will as planned and His will as specifically permitted. If what happens is an evil with no redemptive element, then we must ask if it is for our good (because God permitted it). If God decides something should happen (by permitting it), is that not the same as planning it? If God agrees something should happen but does not plan it, then what does that mean? If, in an attempt to excuse God from planning evil, we say instead that He decides to permit it, doesn't that create more problems? Is God permitting something against His will?

There is one basic question! Does God maintain personal control over what happens to us—*by specific choice?* Can there be any practical difference between "planning" and "permitting"? We don't like to admit it, to put it into words! At its heart, to view our hurting as God's discipline, is a modified form of modern stoicism—with a Christian twist! It can be understood as stoicism planned by God. Is it any wonder that many thinking people reject it as much as humanistic stoicism? (Cf. Chap. 11.)

Yet, thank God there is a better way! We shall see a vital and all-important distinction. God doesn't *send* or *permit*— as a specific, personal choice—our hurting to discipline us! We shall see that instead He stands at our side, often weeping. He can and will lovingly *use* our suffering in a wonderful way if we will open our lives to Him in faith.

Exactly what has God promised to do for us, His redeemed children? With anticipation we look to His Word.

PART III

What Has God Promised?

Dear Father:

We have been thinking about some of the things that make us hurt and have looked at the ways so many of us try to handle them. We have seen that none of these "answers" bring real and lasting peace. Is it because we have not been listening to You? There are so many voices in our world today. We want to know what You have promised us. We are sure that in the midst of our hurting, You have something important to say to us—and do for us! We want to be sure to recognize Your voice and workings. It might surprise us and not be what we have expected. Help us to open our hearts and lives to the faithful ministry of Your Spirit. Sometimes it is hard to patiently wait, but we are trying. In our Savior's name.   *Amen.*

All of us have our own ideas of what God has promised to do for us when we hurt! But have we ever given careful thought to those ideas? What are the implications?

In what way is God involved in our daily lives? Does He oversee everything that happens to us, determining every exact detail? Or, does God assign a guardian angel to watch over us? What would such "care" do to our freedom as persons? Is it possible for us to be really free, and for God at the same time to have total control of life's circumstances? To what extent are we responsible for what comes into our lives? What would it do to our faith to think of God limiting himself? Exactly what can God do when we are hurting? What has He *promised* to do for us, in His Word?

Such questions are almost endless. But we *must* face them if we are going to find His help. Too often we have missed God's gracious and loving care *because of wrong ideas.* In fact, we can even aggravate our suffering by mistaken expectations. As we understand "what God has promised," it will enable us to prove in our lives that His grace *is* sufficient.

18

What's on the Computer?

It was many years ago, long before our amazing modern computers were developed. I had taken a church scouting group on a field trip to the busy railroad yards in Boston. They enjoyed themselves, climbing in and out and over the big switching engine. When we were taken to the control room for the maze of converging tracks, the boys were bored but I was fascinated. One entire wall was a massive map and before it sat several men working switches. Different-colored lights were flashing on the wall map. Our guide explained that every train on every track, for miles in and out of Boston, was kept under constant surveillance. Carefully the trains were directed to the proper tracks to bring them safely to their destination.

Is this your mental picture of how God operates His universe? Is every move of every person monitored? Does God control, by plan or specific permission, the activities of all earth's teeming billions? Of course we are thinking in human terms! How else can we think? More in keeping with modern sophisticated technology, does God lay out a computer program for every life—for every day?

There are some serious problems with such a view. As we have seen, mishaps do occur, and we hurt. We might think of God as only responsible for what happens to those who belong to Him. All the others just have to take the consequences because they are on their own. Thus tragedy, for them, is tough luck, since they refused their opportunities to be protected by God. Such an attitude would be callously hardhearted—and doesn't sound very much like a loving God. Furthermore, this view leaves a lot of questions.

Joe was a helicopter pilot in Vietnam and flew several hundred combat missions. Even though hundreds of his companions lost their lives or were placed in cruel prison camps, Joe returned safely home. His parents, good friends of mine, are certain his life was spared because they had fasted and prayed for his safety. But what about the hundreds of other praying parents whose sons did not escape? What was wrong with their prayers?

It is all right to view God as lovingly operating a celestial computer *when all goes well.* We complete a dangerous journey, or just a normal trip, and we thank Him for traveling mercies on the highway. A near accident occurs, and we are certain that God has graciously protected us. Our plans are changed, and the plane we were to take crashes with the loss of many lives. That is fine and wonderful *for us.* But what about the others less fortunate?

What about the time when an accident does occur to us? The pavement was wet and slippery on the Tulsa bypass. A car careened out of control and crossed the median strip. Tim Green, a young professor-preacher, was killed and his vital ministry was brought to a screeching halt. Behind was left a brokenhearted wife and two children who very much needed a father. George and Jack, two quartet members, were also killed. Grief-stricken parents struggled to adjust to the loss of their children. An entire college community was left in sad shock.

What went wrong? We can't explain this as punishment or discipline. What possible purpose could God have in planning, or specifically permitting, such a tragedy? Yet, if this is our view of God, we must face this question and answer it! To be sure, we can't and don't need to understand the "why" of all that happens in life! To insist otherwise is futile and even foolish. God's ways and workings *are* mysterious! We must learn to accept in faith the unanswerable. That is one of the crucial lessons for us from Jesus' struggle in Gethsemane— "My Father, if it is possible . . . yet not as I will, but as Thou wilt" (Matt. 26:39). *But if we think God is responsible for what happens, that is another matter.* In some tragedies we can have faith that God has a gracious purpose, although unknown to us. Is this possible in *every* tragedy?

Yet, must we see God as *personally* involved in what happens to us? Of course, He could stop adversity or He would not be God. But does that have to mean that it is His will, planned or specifically permitted? Is there no alternative answer? Must our suffering be aggravated by making it His will? Should we pray and ask God to protect us and keep us from tragedy? If we do so, does it not assume He controls it? What has God promised? Does He say that He will be a *protecting* Providence?

Let us search on for *His* answer.

19

A Heavenly Bodyguard

An ancient legend tells of a king who had to send his only son on a long and dangerous journey. He feared greatly for his safety. So he offered a huge prize for the best plan that would protect his son on the trip. Many responded with elaborate suggestions, and the king finally eliminated all but three. One plan was to send the king's armies before the son and destroy any potential enemy. But the king realized that this could not guarantee his son's safety. It would be relatively easy for an individual, or even a small band of terrorists, to escape capture and make an attack from ambush. A second plan was to have the army accompany the son on his journey. But the king knew well that in the confusion of battle his son might be left unguarded. One wise counselor devised a third plan that pleased the king. He suggested that the king select the strongest and bravest warrior in all the kingdom. Then, incognito, the two would make the journey together. In the event that they were discovered, and the king's son was in danger, he would be defended by his bodyguard at the cost of his own life.

Many times our picture of God's protection is more like a personal bodyguard than an impersonal Providence. In recent years this companion has been often identified as our own *special angel.* When we become a Christian, God assigns an angel to us, and he jealously watches over us by day and night.

One Sunday morning my Sunday School class was discussing the matter of angelic protection. Alex spoke up and dramatically described how late one night he fell asleep at the wheel of his car. Suddenly, in the nick of time, he awoke and managed to barely miss the tree toward which his car was plunging. He was certain that his angel had protected him. But while he was relating the story, I glanced across the room at his wife. Alice sat with her head bowed—in sadness. I am sure she was thinking of the time Alex had been in a tragic accident that left him permanently disabled. That is the heart of the problem. Everything is fine when nothing happens, but what about the times when it does? Where is the angel then?

That is precisely the difficulty in thinking that God provides each of His children with a heavenly bodyguard. We come right back to the same problem. When tragedy comes, either the angel is guilty of negligence or the adversity was planned or permitted.

We can even think of the Holy Spirit in these terms. Jesus said that if He returned to the Father, He would send the "Paraclete"; I like to call Him our "Comforter-Helper." He, the Holy Spirit, would dwell *in* us, Jesus promised, as our constant Companion. There were many ministries He would have—our Teacher, Guide, Advocate, etc. But did Jesus ever say He would protect us and keep us from experiencing adversity? Rather than this being so, Jesus warned us of the *opposite.* In the very context of His promise to send the Holy Spirit (cf. John 15:26-27; 16:7-11) He said:

> "These things I have spoken to you, that you may be kept from stumbling. They will make you outcasts from the synagogue; but an hour is coming for everyone who

kills you to think that he is offering service to God. And these things they will do, because they have not known the Father, or Me. But these things I have spoken to you, that when their hour comes, you may remember that I told you of them. And these things I did not say to you at the beginning, because I was with you" *(John 16:1-4)*.

What has God promised? One problem is that the suggestion of a protecting Providence, even angelic care, *is found in parts* of the Old Testament.

A thousand may fall at your side, ten thousand at your right hand; but it will not come near you. You will only look with your eyes and see the recompense of the wicked. Because you have made the Lord your refuge, the Most High your habitation, no evil shall befall you, no scourge come near your tent. For he will give his angels charge of you to guard you in all your ways. On their hands they will bear you up, lest you dash your foot against a stone. You will tread on the lion and the adder, the young lion and the serpent you will trample under foot *(Ps. 91:7-13, RSV)*.

However, you don't have to read much of the Old Testament, even about David, to realize that adversity *did* come into the lives of the people of God. Then what does this mean? Such passages as quoted above reflect the fundamental Jewish doctrine of the *total* or *complete* sovereignty of God. It did not distinguish between *purpose* and *result,* because God is the basic Cause of everything.[1]

Further, there are in the Old Testament some examples of the very ancient idea that adversity is evidence that the victim has personally sinned. Behind such a view is the *necessity* of God protecting the faithful from adversity. But as early as the Book of Job this tragically erroneous concept was challenged by some and rejected (cf. Chap. 12). Yet, sadly, remnants of this fallacious belief persisted, and Jesus had to correct the error more than once. His disciples questioned whether a man was born blind because of his or his parents' sin (cf. John 9:2-3). On another occasion Jesus assured His disciples that the Galileans who had been murdered by Pilate were not greater sinners than their fellow countrymen who escaped death. Similarly, He pointed out that the 18 unfortunate souls who were killed when the Tower of Siloam fell on them were no worse "culprits" than the rest of the inhabitants of Jerusalem (cf. Luke 13:1-5). Even today the same idea is contained in the oft-heard question: "What did I [he] do to deserve that?"

We will search in vain for any New Testament promise that when we become a Christian, God will watch over us *in the sense of protection from adversity.* He does not promise to control what happens to us by either an impersonal Providence or a heavenly bodyguard. The devil sought to trip up Jesus at this very point, using the ancient promise from Psalm 91, yet out of its context (cf. Matt. 4:5-7).[2] But Jesus wisely resisted his insidious designs. Perhaps it comes as a surprise to us, but plainly stated—*God does not assume responsibility for whether or not adversity comes into our lives!*

Our suffering need not be intensified by the painful thought that God is involved in its coming. He did not cause or condone it. Instead, He suffers with us! If we can get this clear in our thinking, it will spare us many unnecessary heartaches. We can bear our trials with a braver faith and a brighter hope. So we look further for what God *does* promise.

20

Who Done It?

If God is not involved in the adversity that *comes* into our lives, *then what determines it?* Or is it determined at all? There have always been those who consider themselves to be the children of fate (cf. Chap. 10). If God does not control what happens to us, are we any better off? What causes evil or adversity anyway?

There are, of course, obvious *human* causes for tragedies. Sue knew that the railing on the second-floor balcony needed replacing, and had neglected to take care of it. One night, at a party, she accidentally leaned heavily against the railing, and she and a companion both plunged to the ground below. Now, confined to a wheelchair with paralysis from a broken back, it is only human for her to wonder why God should have allowed this to happen. But should God be blamed? What did He have to do with it?

Very early in my ministry I encountered this quite dramatically. Repeatedly Bill had been told to not smoke in the garage where he worked. But one morning, before the boss arrived, he was "enjoying" a smoke. He casually flipped the end of the cigarette into a can containing gasoline. It flared up, and when Bill tried to stamp out the fire, the gas fumes ignited his clothing. In a moment his body was a flaming torch. Only the quick action of a passing motorist saved his life. There were endless months of agonizing suffering as he battled for life. At times the pain was so intense he lost contact with reality.

I shall never forget the numberless visits I made in hospitals, sanitariums, and mental institutions. More than one person asked me how a loving God could permit such suffering. But why blame God? What did He have to do with it?

We all know of incidents of this kind. Many adversities have a direct human cause. The list of these causes is long: carelessness, neglect, indifference, foolishness, thoughtlessness, daring, defiance, stubbornness, stupidity, etc. When tragedy comes, why should God be blamed?

But all adversities do not have such obvious causes. We would really have no serious problem if that were the case. A friend, knowing of what I was attempting to write, told me recently: "Most people cause their own problems." I am afraid he has not opened his eyes to a hurting world! Perhaps his attitude stems from the fact that *thus far* "the lines have fallen to [him] in pleasant places" (Ps. 16:6). With his affluence and comfortable circumstances, he hasn't really hurt.

How well I remember my agnostic doctor, partly in jest, asking: "Why do I need God? I have all the money I can reasonably use. I and my family are in good health." From his vantage point of success he felt very much that he was the master of his own fate. My answer, as a fledgling pastor, was simply that life for him was not over yet, and that one day he would learn the answer. Before he died, a broken man, his wife had spent many years in a mental institution. He gambled away his resources and lost his medical practice in disgrace.

But we have seen that many people deeply hurt because of adversities for which they have no personal responsibility.

Death comes, sudden or prolonged, from disease, accident, natural disaster, or war. Financial security or health is suddenly lost. We suffer the bitter loss of friendships or a marriage. Children break our hearts. Or the inevitable loneliness and uselessness of old age overtakes us. The sources of such hurts are almost endless.

But what is the cause? Is it because God plans or specifically permits the hurting? What does He have to do with it? *Are we not really asking: Why doesn't God intervene?* Why doesn't He, out of loving compassion, break the laws of His universe? Have we ever stopped to think what that would mean? Atmospheric conditions would not spawn hurricanes. When a fault in the earth shifts, God would steady the quaking earth. If we are bitten by a poisonous snake, the venom would be neutralized. Two objects *could* occupy the same space at the same time. The law of gravity would have to be constantly set aside. The list could go on and on.

But is that the kind of a world we want—*for everybody?* Or is it the kind of world we would like—*for us?* Really, what kind of a world would we have if God *promiscuously* canceled His laws to say nothing of Him doing so *in a preferential manner?*

Why do things happen as they do? The very simple answer is the law of cause and effect. For every effect there is a cause—somewhere. We are not in the hands of fate. Neither do we experience the designs of a Celestial Dictator, even though He be lovingly compassionate.

Have we ever thought of what it would mean for God to arbitrarily control everything that happens to us? If He exercised such control, then we would be nothing more than puppets, mechanical robots, manipulated by God's computer. Is that what we want? I seriously doubt it.

Who done it? Sometimes we did! But more often it is a matter of us living in a world controlled by cause and effect.

On occasions it appears that we are victims of a cruel cause, but it is not designed personally by God or devils. Would we really want it to be different?

21

God Tied His Hands

One day I found a baby robin fluttering and hopping in the grass under a large maple tree. I reached down to put it back in the nest that was nearby. But there was a sudden screech from the mother robin, who was sitting on one of the branches, unseen by me. It was as if she was scolding me for interfering in something that was none of my business. So I went on my way and left that mother with her all-important training task. Evidently one of her children had been a slow learner, and she finally had pushed it out of the nest. After fluttering to the ground, the infant had still not learned that robins are meant to fly! Here was a mother with an aching heart (if bird's hearts ache). Can you imagine what life would be like to that robin if it never learned to fly?

I have counseled many a parent who never learned that simple lesson. Without doubt, the most difficult period of parenthood is when our children are "testing their wings." But if they are ever to become *real persons*, they must be given their freedom—*at the right time*. Unfortunately, it is not always clear, for parent or child, exactly when that time is. Yet, although it is often painful, we *must* let our children learn the lessons of personal responsibility, *and keep our hands off*. How much we want, even as when they took their first toddling footsteps, to reach out and "help" them. But the wise parent knows this would not be a help but a hindrance. We all have seen the consequences of being tied to Mother's apron strings. The effects often continue into marriage and even down to old age. Some people never do grow up! *True personhood requires free and responsible action.*

Who knows this better than God? From all eternity He has had angelic beings that were created to serve Him—*automatically.* Their obedience does not involve freedom or choice. It is compulsive and determined. *Their relationship with God cannot be based on love,* in any meaningful sense. But God *is* love and love *must* have a response. So He made man—you and me.

In order for us to be real persons, capable of true love, we must be free. The only way for us to be free is for God to be limited. In our understanding, it is impossible for God to have *absolute* power and at the same time for us to have freedom. We can't put the two together. The two seem mutually exclusive, because one cancels out the other. If God's power is unlimited, we cannot be free. If we are free, God cannot have unlimited power. *It is as simple as that!*

But we know God has absolute power, or else He wouldn't be God! *Did He not limit himself?* Could it not be that God *chose* to limit His power in order that we might be free and experience true personhood? If that is so, then God has tied His own hands! This is the awesome and frightening step He took when He created man. But could there be any other way? How else could we be truly free and love God? Otherwise our love would only be compulsive.[1] Would that be love?

Instead of *self-limitation* being an evidence of weakness, it is the *finest* kind of strength. We can see this even in our limited human experience. It is easier to do some tasks than to stand by and permit someone else to do them, perhaps

87

less efficiently. Tom was an exceptionally able layman in my church. There were few skills in the building trade he could not do with expertise. Yet he had a most difficult time working with the other laymen on our church building. Repeatedly I've seen him take a tool from one of their hands, a bit impatiently, and do the job himself. It was harder for him to *let them do it* than to do it himself. Yet if he had permitted them to do their job, even with less efficiency, *they would have learned how.*

However, making a person is much different than constructing a building! We can only become a true person if we have the *freedom to do it ourselves.* I wonder how many times God has wanted to take the tool out of my hands? But He knows better and has tied His hands. This is evidence of *greater* strength and love.

So, God created man free and put him into this world governed by such fundamental laws as cause and effect, gravity, and many more. God limited himself to the extent that He will respect those laws and not violate or interfere with them. We are also subject to these laws! I am not sure when I first heard it, or who said it. But one of the most searching truths I know is: "We are free to do as we choose, but we are not free to choose the consequences of our choice." We are free to jump out of a 10th-story window, but we can't choose if we will stand still, fall up, or fall down. Our problem is that we want to be free to "do our own thing." But then we want to blame God when things go wrong. We can't have both, freedom and divine responsibility.

Of course, we know what happened. The creation of man with freedom was a solemn risk. Man *could* choose to reject God, and that is exactly what happened. He was free to usurp the sovereign *control* over his life that God had designed for himself. We need to clearly understand the difference between freedom and sovereignty. A dictionary will tell us that freedom is the *power of choice* and sovereignty is the *power of control.* Man used his freedom to take control of his own life. The consequences of that fatal choice are still unfolding. I am convinced that *the cause for every evil,* even what we call natural evil, stems from what man has done to himself and his world as the result of rejecting the Lordship of God. We sing: "This is my Father's world." But the evil in this world is of man's own making! God does not create or cause evil—*of any kind.*

A refreshing new approach, at least to me, to this problem of the ages is given by a newly converted lawyer, in legal language. God gave us dominion over the earth, making us *His agents* through creation (Gen. 1:26-30). In legal terms, the "theory of agency" is freedom of action beyond that of a mechanical robot or servant. The *agent* is authorized to act within the *scope of his authority,* which has set limits. God laid out in Scripture the limits of our authority. However, at the same time we were given free will by God. *Without* this free will we are not a free agent, but *with* free will we can defy the limits of our authority. This is what sometimes happens in civil law. The agent exceeds his authority. Thus, it is man's abuse of the authority given to him by God that creates the preponderance of human grief. It is *one* answer to why a good God presides over such an evil world.[2]

Now we can see more clearly our predicament. God has tied His hands and will not interfere in the natural course of life in this world. Because of man's sin we hurt—directly or remotely. The *source* of our hurting is not God. He is not to blame. Why does He not stop it from happening if He truly loves us? It is because He has tied His hands in order that we might be free and love Him as real persons.

22

Ever Hear God Cry?

"God doesn't even care! How could He care and allow me to hurt like this?" It is easy to come to this conclusion. We find it hard to put together a God of love and compassion with human suffering. It seems like a contradiction. If God has limited himself so that He can't, or won't, stop us from hurting, doesn't that have to mean that He doesn't really care? How often this question is asked, many times with bitterness. The songwriter asked:

> Does Jesus care when my heart is pained
> Too deeply for mirth and song,
> As the burdens press, and the cares distress,
> And the way grows weary and long?
>
> Does Jesus care when my way is dark
> With a nameless dread and fear?
> As the daylight fades into deep night shades,
> Does He care enough to be near?

Then he answered:

> Oh, yes, He cares; I know He cares.
> His heart is touched with my grief.
> When the days are weary, the long nights dreary,
> I know my Savior cares.
>
> —FRANK E. GRAEFF

Yes, God cares very much—*at the deepest level.* He truly *sympathizes* with us. The basic meaning of *sympathy* is "sameness of feeling" which enables one person to enter into another's feelings and emotions. This is real compassion for the suffering and trouble of others.

Is this not true in human experience? Who can help us most when we hurt? Is it not the person who has known a similar heartache and possesses a "sameness of feeling"?

Pastor Peterson told me how he once was attempting to comfort two grieving parents after their son was killed in an auto accident. Suddenly the mother, overcome by her grief, blurted out: "It is all right for you to sit there and talk of God's love and comfort when it is my son and not yours who is dead!" There was nothing the pastor could say in answer to that embittered outburst. He sadly left, unable to minister to Mr. and Mrs. Clark. It was only a short time later that one of Pastor Peterson's own sons was stricken with a ruptured appendix and died within a few hours. After the funeral, even before the brokenhearted pastor-father returned home, he went to visit the Clarks. Sitting in the same chair, he said to Mrs. Clark: "*Now* I can tell you about God's love and comfort when a son is suddenly taken away." He could sympathize because he had the "sameness of feeling."

Have you not found it so? When you have been hurting, has not your greatest comfort come from someone who has had a similar experience? Who can sympathize most with us when our heart aches over a straying child? Is it not the one who also has had a prodigal? As you stand by and helplessly watch an aged parent painfully die "by inches," it is the person who has borne the same burden that can best understand. It is no wonder that blind and handicapped volunteers, who have conquered their trials, provide the best therapy to one who suffers a similar affliction.

But how does God sympathize with us? Does He actually feel our hurts? The answer is a resounding "YES." This is a vital part of the Incarnation, when God became man in Christ. The central truth of the Incarnation is *God's total identification with us.* He stepped down and placed (lit. "stood") His love beside us when we were yet sinners (Rom. 5:8). We know that, as our Savior, He was totally identified with our sin. "He made Him who knew no sin *to be* sin on our behalf, that we might become the righteousness of God in Him" (2 Cor. 5:21). This could only take place through *His* death for *our* sins. But God was identified with man *in Christ's life as well as in His death.* A vital part of the Good News (gospel) is that God suffered in Christ *everything* that we can possibly experience (Heb. 2:18). The result is that He can "sympathize with our weaknesses" (4:15). In other words, God knows by experience how we hurt. He has the "sameness of feeling."

What can this mean, other than that when we hurt, He hurts too? When we weep, He also weeps. If *human* love is expressed by "weeping with those who weep" (cf. Rom. 12:15), how much more must *divine* love be evidenced by sympathizing tears as He shares our sorrows? In the blackness of our Gethsemane He can slip a comforting arm around us *because He has been there.* In fact, He will be so close we can sense His sobs. Have you ever heard God cry? I am sure He has wept with me many times.

Why is God's sympathizing presence so important to us in our hurting? It is because there is a point beyond which human companionship cannot go. Although friends and loved ones *try* to share our sorrows, their compassion is limited. No man can *fully* understand another man's sorrow, and eventually we reach the place of "aloneness" in our heartache. It is here that God would make real His caring companionship.

Several years ago I was the guest of Ken and Louise. Along with their two lovely children they warmly welcomed me into their family circle. As a result, our two families became close friends, visiting each other on vacations. Then tragedy suddenly struck. Although he was only in his 40s, Ken was fatally stricken with a heart attack. It was impossible for us to attend the funeral, but soon afterward my wife and I visited Louise. In fact, it was on my arm that she made her first return visit to the new grave. Seeing my anxious face, Louise quietly smiled and said: "It is all right, He is here."

That night Louise *tried* to explain her experience. Throughout the agonizing hours that became days, the shocking discovery, the police investigation (because of the sudden death), the funeral arrangements and services, she was in a state of shock. Decisions were made and duties performed, but in a perfunctory manner. She couldn't think or feel. Just the night before we arrived, she seemed to regain her normal faculties. It was then she became aware of the Divine Presence all about her. He was closer than any earthly friend or loved one and was *constantly* there. On her sad face there was a distinct heavenly glow.

Does Jesus care? I know He cares! He who wept with two sisters before their brother's tomb stands with us in our deepest hurts and weeps again.

23

What *Can* God Do?

If God has not promised to protect us from adversity, then what has He promised to do? Isaiah voiced God's promise: "Do not fear, for I am with you" (41:10). "When you pass through the waters, I will be with you" (43:2).

This takes on deeper meaning in the New Testament when the risen Christ promised: "Lo, I am with you always" (Matt. 28:20). He had explained this to His disciples the night before the Cross, but they could not understand. When it became apparent that He was leaving, the disciples were understandably troubled and distressed. Jesus told them He would not leave them as orphans (John 14:18) but would send the Holy Spirit to them *in a new way*. The Holy Spirit had been *with* them (in Jesus), but now He would be *in* them (v. 17). As a result, the Holy Spirit would be with them forever (v. 16). In this new way, in the person of the Holy Spirit, Jesus would come to them and remain with them constantly (v. 18).

Thus God has promised to be with us, even in us, throughout all of the experiences of life. This includes the times of adversity and hurting. What does His presence within us mean to us? It certainly means *strength,* sufficient strength for every need and circumstance of life. This was

God's promise to Paul when he asked God to remove his thorn in the flesh, whatever it was. God refused to take away the thorn but instead promised: "My grace is sufficient for you" (2 Cor. 12:9).

It is hard to comprehend the magnitude of this promise of God. *Regardless* of the need we might have, His presence within will provide sufficient strength for us. As I hurriedly drove my car to the home of one of my parishioners, I asked God out loud: "Lord, what can I say to Jane?" It would seem that she had reached the breaking point. She had been in the hospital more than six months during the current year, many times near death with acute asthma. Her only relative in the United States had been lost at sea in a shipwreck. Her husband was causing her all kinds of anxieties. Now, word had just come that her only son had been killed while in the service of his country. What was there to say?

I was surprised to have her husband meet me at the door with a puzzled look on his face. He said: "Since we received word of Jimmy's death, I haven't been an arm's length from Jane's side. I have expected her to collapse at any moment, but something seems to be holding her up." As I gripped his hand, I gently corrected him: "Tom, it is not something but Someone!" God was keeping His promise of sufficient strength.

Amazingly, God has further promised that He "will not allow you to be tested above your powers" (1 Cor. 10:13, NEB).[1] His guarantee is that *whatever* we are experiencing we can handle by His grace. Ruth was hurting, about as much as it is possible to hurt. She looked up at me with haunted eyes and confessed, "It's no use, I can't make it." She was an attractive young nurse who had recently been converted. Sometime before, following major surgery, she had become accidentally addicted to morphine. Now, as a Christian, she felt it was wrong to simply maintain herself from the hospital drug supply. So she had voluntarily admitted herself to the hospital for the painful withdrawal. Within days she looked like a crazed animal in her "barred bed," rather than the neat and fastidious young lady I had known. Now she could stand the agonizing pain no longer and was ready to ask for the merciful relief that morphine would bring.

I whispered to her the promise and guarantee of God— "... not allow ... above your powers ..." A new look came into her eyes and, gripping my wrist until her fingernails literally drew blood, she affirmed, "I can make it now!" And make it she did! The happy day came when she walked out of that hospital on my arm, a free woman.

God will keep His commitment if He has to move heaven and earth (and hell) to do it. He will give us sufficient strength to overcome our trial!

Then why do we fail? Is it not because we do not open ourselves to the strength of His presence? Are not our hearts closed by self-pity and bitterness? All we can see is our hurt. God's voice is drowned out as we scream: "WHY?" All the time He is there waiting and weeping.

As Betty lay in the hospital, still not knowing the full extent of her injuries from an auto accident, her son cried: "Mom, why should this happen to you?" She answered: "Don, I don't ask, 'Why?' but 'What?'" Betty was putting into practice a sermon she heard a few months earlier. I had preached a message on the theme: "The Christian must learn to ask, 'What?' and not 'Why?'" based on Paul's reaction to his confrontation with Christ on the Damascus road (cf. Acts 22:10). Don, whose life had been ruined by rebellion and bitterness, left that hospital room declaring: "If my mom can take that attitude, then I need to find her God." It was the turning point of his life. Not only did Betty find

96

God's strength sufficient for herself, but she led a wandering son back to God.

As we learn to stop blaming God for the hurts of our lives and instead discover His marvelous strengthening grace, how different our lives can be.

But is that *all* God can do, give us strength to endure? Listen! "And we know that God causes all things to work together for good to those who love God, to those who are called according to His purpose" (Rom. 8:28). Undoubtedly this is one of the best-known promises in the New Testament. Yet, it is seldom *really* believed, even by devout Christians.

Some things—yes; *most* things—perhaps; but *all* things—impossible. This is the response of most of us. The *totality* of the promise *is* staggering. God says He will cause everything, *every single thing,* to work together for good. Whose good? Obviously it is for *our* good. There are no exceptions; *everything* that happens to us is included.

But what is meant by "good," our good? It has a lot of different meanings, as the dictionary makes plain. Yet, when Paul voiced God's promise, surely he had some definite things in mind. "Our good" must certainly include what is in our best interests. It is for our *benefit* or *profit.* Can it be good for us if it is not for our advantage? But personal profit *alone* can't be the whole story about "our good," because sometimes what benefits us can be as distasteful as castor oil.

When Paul said that God will cause everything to work together for our good, he doesn't seem to be talking about taking bitter medicine. There must be some measure of *personal satisfaction* in "our good." It is true that *good* experiences are not necessarily *all* pleasant and enjoyable all the time. But neither are they repugnant and unpleasant. In a proper sense we are happy with them.

Still there is another essential element in "our good." It

97

is difficult to define, and we almost instinctively "feel" it. If what happens to us is to be good, it must not only be profitable and pleasant, but also *right*. A good result is always correct. When we view what happens to us, things are "as they should be," if they are good.

As is often the case, we can understand what Paul means by looking at the opposite. The alternative to good is "bad," which is *wrong* as well as unpleasant and not in our best interests.

Does that mean that we can always *see* the good, as it is being worked out by God? Of course not! There are times when we see more than at other times, but *basically* this is a point of faith. God has promised that He will cause everything to work together for our good. The foundation for faith is in the promise of God *and not what we see*. So, in the midst of the darkness, we trust in the promise of God. He is working.

This was beautifully illustrated by Corrie ten Boom, when she was being interviewed by Billy Graham. It was obviously not pleasant for her to relive many of her horrible experiences in a Nazi prison camp during World War II, including the death of her sister. All the time she was speaking, almost unnoticed, a mass of tangled threads was lying on her lap. When she reached the point of praise for the wonderful way God had worked through her tragedy, she turned the tangled threads over and revealed a beautiful piece of tapestry. Effectively, even eloquently, she had given a witness that words could never convey. While she could only see tangled threads, God was weaving a masterpiece. Now it was plain for all to see, but in the prison camp it was seen only by faith.

But what about Corrie's sister? She perished in that horrible prison camp! All can *see* the ever-emerging loveliness of God's working in Corrie's life. But how did God cause that bitter prison camp experience to work together for her sister's good, when she suffered such an untimely death? This is the question that we often face when a loved one dies, especially when the death appears premature or there is prolonged suffering. Sometimes it is "by inches," almost literally, because of brittle diabetes or from a creeping malignancy. Yes, God does give His sufficient strength, but how can this be seen as being for the victim's good? We must face this hard question.

There are some relatively easy answers. Is not death in the Lord the ultimate good? That is certainly true, but is that what Paul is saying here? Also, we can look at the "good" as working out *for others* and not the "victim" himself. But Paul makes it quite clear that it is "to those who love God" and "to those who are called according to His purpose," that the promise is directed. This seems to make it plain that Paul has in mind the person himself and not others who might be involved. Any adequate understanding of God's promise to work things together for good *must* include the eternal dimensions. We shall see that it is vitally related to a further promise that we will examine shortly. However, first some crucial distinctions must be seen.

To recognize that God promises to cause everything to work together for good (I personally prefer the literal Greek—"God works everything together . . .") does *not* mean that He *causes* or *specifically permits* the adversity to happen (cf. Chap. 19). Paul does not say that God considers everything that comes into our lives as being necessary for our good. If that were so, then it must come from God because *all good ultimately comes from God.* Once again let it be said, as we have suggested, that our suffering is not sent or allowed by God. *He has nothing to do with its coming.*

There is a common misunderstanding here. How often we are stricken with tragedy and we conclude that God knows that it is for our good—*intrinsically.* So we struggle to accept it by faith. This was the mistake that Mrs. Jenkins made when, with trembling chin, she said to me: "I will soon be totally blind [in middle age], and I am trying so hard to understand it as being for my good" (cf. Chap. 16). I had just preached on Rom. 8:28, and she had missed the main thrust of my message. I hadn't said, nor had Paul, that our adversities *are* for our good.

Paul is very clear! God does not *cause* (or permit) everything that happens to us, insisting that we accept it as for our good. Instead, He *works together* for good everything that happens to us. *That's a big difference!* The term used by Paul *(sunergeō,* cf. Mark 16:20*)* is very meaningful. It literally means to "work with." Thus the promise is that God will *take* everything that happens to us and *work with it* for our good. God is not responsible for what happens to us. But He will take what happens and work with it. That *is* His promise!

One more thing must be noted. This is not a blanket promise for everyone. It has very clearly stated restrictions. God promises to work with everything that happens and cause it to result in good *to those who love Him and to those who are called according to His purpose. Only* when we love Him, and to love Him is to serve Him, can we expect Him to work things together. We know what it means to love Him, but what is the significance of "those who are called"? Fortunately the immediate context (vv. 29-30) tells us that our "calling" and "predestination," as well as our "justification" and "glorification," are all tied up together. We are "predestined to become conformed to the image of His Son, that He might be the first-born among many brethren" (v. 29). The "called according to His purpose" are those who are seeking to be like Christ.

So, God's wonderful promise (v. 28) is limited to those

who love and serve Him and to those who aspire to be Christlike. It is for them that God will work everything for good. Does that not make sense? If we love ourselves more than God and have no desire to be like Christ, how could God work everything for our good without violating our personhood? It is sad indeed to see a worldling try to find comfort in this promise for God's children, when his world is falling apart.

But the end is not yet! In this same chapter (Romans 8) Paul stated another dimension of God's promise to His hurting children. After describing every imaginable adversity (vv. 35-36, 38-39), Paul assured the Roman believers that none of these things could separate them from the love of Christ (vv. 35, 39). "But in [lit. "in the midst of"] all these things we overwhelmingly conquer through Him who loved us" (v. 37). The translation "overwhelmingly conquer" rather weakly expresses Paul's cry of confidence.[2] This is one of those words Paul created to express the inexpressible (cf. 5:20). He took the word for "conquer" *(nikaō)* and added a prefix *(huper)* which means "over and above, beyond, more than." What can it mean to be *overconquerors* or to be *more than a conqueror?*

Many years ago I was privileged to hear E. Stanley Jones, the great Methodist missionary-scholar, preach on this verse. In response to the question of what it could possibly mean, he gave an inspired answer. To conquer is to endure, stand triumphantly, and overcome in the face of adversity. It means to overcome our trial. But to *overconquer means to start a counter good.* Jesus not only endured the Cross and overcame it by the Resurrection, but He *overconquered.* From that Cross has flowed the unending stream of redemption.

So, we are more than conquerors *only* if, beyond our endurance of and triumph over suffering, a counter good comes forth. The magnitude of the promise of God is breathtaking. In our trial He promises to stand with us and give us strength to endure and overcome. Beyond that we have His promise that He will work with everything that comes into our lives and will shape even the most difficult situation into that which is for our good.

On that dark day in the 40s when Peter Marshall fell victim to a fatal heart attack, who could have envisioned what would take place? The chaplain of the United States Senate, the popular, young preacher whose searching sermons were heard by thousands, the spiritual counselor to an uncounted multitude—was now dead! How could it be right? He was in the prime of life with a glorious ministry before him. How utterly tragic! What possible good could come from this? But a shocked and frightened young widow opened her heart to God with faith in His promises. From that Spirit-quickened heart began to flow a stream of inspired writing. First a printing of Peter's prayers and sermons, then his biography, then a window into her heart that revealed her struggle and triumph, and then volume after volume of spiritual treasure.

Looking back, we can already see! Instead of thousands hearing Peter, multitudes have been deeply touched by his life. The half has not been seen, let alone told, of the multiplied millions who have been blessed by the pen of Catherine. Yes, we can see in action God's promise to strengthen us with sufficient grace in life's most difficult hours. We can see God working together the most tragic events so that all the world can see the "good" result. Even more, we see how God is able to create a redemptive stream that flows out of the dark abyss of tragic and premature death.

But have we enough faith to see that all this was *even for Peter's good?* Is this not the deepest meaning of God's promise to work everything together for *our* good, even though we lose our lives? Can we believe that, although this earthly life ends, in the hands of a loving God our death may be the fertile garden in which He can bring to fruitage a bountiful eternal harvest? Would that not be for *our* good?

God does not promise to protect us from adversity. Neither does He send or permit tragedy to come into our lives, supposedly for our good. But He does promise to come to us, when we hurt, with sufficient strength. If we will trust Him, He will work everything together for our good. Greatest of all, even from what we men call tragedy, He would shine forth a bright beacon of help and hope to those around us.

24

Deo Volente

When was the last time you received a letter that included some plans which closed with the strange letters "D.V."? This was once commonplace in correspondence among Christians. Tom, a friend of mine in Oklahoma City, got such a letter from his preacher-father. It stated that he would be arriving for a visit on a certain day about 3 p.m., "D.V." So Tom promptly checked the bus terminal, the train station, and the airport. He was embarrassed when he found out what "D.V." meant.

I carefully explained to my New Testament class that "D.V." was an abbreviation for the Latin words *"Deo Volente."* The translation of the Latin expression was: "God willing." I suggested that it would be a good idea to remember it because they would meet it on the final exam. At least two or three still gave the answer that "D.V." meant "God is violent."

How does our conclusion, that God does not arbitrarily determine all that *comes* into our lives, relate to this New Testament concept? There are several different expressions that convey this same basic idea—"God willing."[1] Plans are made or journeys are set up *subject* to the will or permission of God.

Does this *necessarily* indicate the existence of a Divine Providence that *orders* all of the events of life? Thus any plans that are made must be submitted for God's approval or they face the prospect of being overruled and canceled. Was this the spirit in which Paul and James "bowed" to God's will? Did they view God as an *Absolute Sovereign,* who ruled His universe and all the persons in it, with autocratic control? Is this a *true* picture of God, even if His rule is one of loving concern?

Only James gives us an insight into the significance of the expression "God willing." The worldling blissfully makes his plans with no thought of the precarious nature of life. In contrast, realizing that life is as tenuous as a puff of steam, we should face the future with the spirit of "God willing" (cf. Jas. 4:13-16). James makes it clear, as do the other references, that the attitude of "God willing" relates to *making plans for the future.* Our personal choice is involved. It is not describing our reaction to God's arbitrary sovereign control of all of the events in our lives.

However, for us to condition our actions in this way— "God willing"—*does* indicate our *recognition of divine sovereignty.*

This is one basic difference between the worldling and the Christian. While so many *try* to act in independent self-sufficiency, even arrogance, the human race teeters on the brink of total self-destruction. It is only prudent and sane to respect the authority and power of God as we live in this explosive world. The child of God has acknowledged His sovereignty and conditions all of his activity by this recognition.

But the expression "God willing" speaks of much more than His sovereignty. It is also *an expression of our dependence upon God.* In reality, when we say, "the Lord willing" we will do this or that, we *mean* that will be the case *if*

He helps us. I think the greatest curse of our day is self-sufficiency, which leads to independence, which is sin! The moment we think we can live without God, we have sinned! This little expression is a confession that without Him we can do nothing. We are totally dependent upon Him.

Beyond that, when we confess, "If God wills," we are *renewing a pledge of obedience.* In substance we mean that if He is *not willing,* we will not do it. This must be the constant spirit of the faithful believer. Any and all of our desires and plans are always subject to His will. "Not my will, but His, be done" is not only a crisis decision but also a constant attitude.

So this little "Christian expression," as I like to call it, does not represent slavish obedience to an overruling Divine Providence. Instead it is the response of a fully committed heart. He is Sovereign of our hearts and lives. We are totally dependent on Him. Our every act or deed, and hopefully our thoughts, is gratefully under His loving Lordship. Therefore, when we use the phrase "God willing," it in no way denies that God has given to us meaningful freedom and personhood.

25

Can't God Lead Us?

Bill came rushing into my office with great concern on his face. "Prof, I need help!" After calming him down a bit, I learned the problem. Bill was only two weeks away from graduation and was ready to start his assignment as a social worker in Detroit. But in recent weeks an increasing sense of uncertainty had gripped him. He had a nagging question that almost haunted him. "I wonder if God is calling me to preach." Bill was a deeply committed Christian, and there was no hesitation about doing God's will. All that he wanted to know was His will.

My first response was one I often make, which generally comes as a surprise. "Bill, God wants you to know His will *more than you do.*" We didn't have much time because, if God was calling Bill into the ministry, he would have to make an immediate and drastic change in his plans. It would be necessary to return to school (in two weeks) for the ministerial course of studies. So we covenanted with each other to pray for God's definite direction, and he agreed to come back to see me in a week. But before the appointed time, Bill came bounding into my office again. This time his face was beaming. "It's wonderful, Prof! I *know* now I should continue my plans to go to Detroit and take the job as a social worker." A letter from Bill, a few months later, confirmed the correctness of his decision. He was happily engaged in his new labors.

One of a Christian's greatest joys is the *certainty* of God's leadership in his life. As I sit writing this chapter, I can look back over more than 40 years of following Christ. How wonderful has been His guidance! Sometimes it has been in *big* decisions—ministerial call, college, life's companion, pastorates, graduate studies, full-time teaching, evangelism, etc. Other times it has been in *small* things too trivial to mention here. Often I have said, in preaching and counseling, if the night I was saved I had been given a blank sheet of paper and told to write on it my greatest desires, I could not have begun to imagine what God has given to me. But isn't that exactly what God has promised to do? (Cf. 1 Cor. 2:9.)

When we speak of God not specifically causing what comes into our lives, this might be misunderstood to mean that He can't lead and guide us. There could be nothing further from the truth. Unfortunately, there are those who only think of divine guidance in terms of escaping from tragedy or discovering a great bonanza. They were suddenly impressed to not take a certain plane, and the flight ended in disaster with all aboard being killed. Or they had a strong feeling they should make a certain investment, and they "hit it rich." I suppose there *could have been* divine guidance involved, though this also happens to people who have no thought of God and are only playing a hunch. Certainly the leadership of God is more meaningful than to be limited to such traumatic experiences.

The *full* picture of God's guidance is only seen over the long run. Oh, yes, God leads us in small details and in what might appear as insignificant matters. But it takes a broader perspective to fully appreciate His leadership. *God's direc-*

tions follow a pattern and plan. A small segment does not give us a true view of the design. What we see, because it is partial, might even appear distorted. Also, many times God is leading us when we are least aware of it.

Instead of God's guidance being an overpowering compulsion, it is a *response* to our earnest entreaty. *He only guides those who seek His leadership.* That is why divine guidance, in its deepest meaning, is fully compatible with God's self-limitation. Most Christians recognize that, as a normal thing, God does not promise to *safeguard* His children from adversity and even tragedy. We shall see in the next section that there are exceptions to that norm. The evidence of His leadership is *not* the absence of calamity but the *end result.* We have seen what God can and will do when we hurt (cf. Chap. 23). God's guidance is seen when, in response to our faith and obedience, He works everything together for our good.

God has a wonderful pattern or design for each of our lives. He wants us to discover and work out that plan. He won't impose it upon us but will wonderfully work *with* us as we seek His leadership and enabling strength. The fact that He respects our freedom and personhood and does not arbitrarily determine what happens to us, in no way destroys the joyous assurance that He is leading and guiding our lives. There is nothing that pleases God more than to respond to our genuine desire for His direction. Yet, we must always remember that divine guidance is *never* imposed upon us, but is *always* in answer to our fervent appeal.

26

Isn't God in Control?

Ultimately this is the question we have to ask and answer! If we accept the self-limitation of God, making Him *not responsible* for everything that *comes* into our lives, does that mean He has relinquished control of His universe? Without question that would be a horrible and unthinkable conclusion. The real issue is, What do we mean by *control?*

Have you realized that in recent years there has been a remarkable interest in puppetry? It does not all relate to children's shows like "Sesame Street." Increasingly there is a more subtle and sophisticated humor as in "Kukla, Fran, and Ollie" and the very popular "Muppet Show," on which many big-name stars reportedly want to perform. Even among religious groups there is an increased demand for the puppet ministry. Probably there are some psychological reasons for this modern taste if we are wise enough to discover them. We do know that the adult mind shows a surprising interest in what is supposed to be children's material.[1] Maybe it is a subconscious escape from, or even revolt against, the overdose of violence that fills modern life. Another possibility is that the world of dolls gives to us a sense of security in a very insecure world.

Regardless of *why* there is this modern interest in puppetry, the puppets depict *one type of control.* Everything they do is determined by a string or wire. Nothing is left to chance and everything is controlled. There are those who are only comfortable with this kind of control. It need not be a wire, but it can be control of another kind, like a closed creed or regulated conduct. Such control offers one type of security. It is a security that comes with no human responsibility. Some even insist that this is the only way that our salvation is secure, making God *totally* responsible. But the security that such control brings destroys our freedom and personhood. Are we then any more than puppets? If this is what we mean by "control," then God *did* surrender it when He limited himself in order to make us persons.

But what is the significance of the earliest Christian confession, "Jesus is Lord!" Does it mean that we surrender our freedom and accept the role of puppets? No! We are still very much persons. But we *use* our freedom to give Him control of our lives, not as puppets but persons. We are committed to His will. He is in control as He leads and guides our lives. (Cf. Chap. 25.)

If God doesn't control or determine all that happens to us, even as Christians, then what does His Lordship and control mean? Perhaps it is best described as God having control, not over what happens to us, *but over what happens next.* To say it another way, He does not determine *what* happens to us, but as our Lord, He determines *what we do with what happens to us.* This is control that does not demean us as persons. Further, it offers us security that is as certain as God himself. It is the security of a *personal relationship* and not a *prison house.*

Yes, God *is* in control! And His is the greatest kind of control. From all eternity He was concerned to *control persons.* This was possible only by relinquishing, for a time, the *control of things.* Now He has the control that freedom and personhood make possible. Is there a better way to describe it than *the control of love?* As He controls our hearts, the *bonds of love* produce a quality and spontaneity of response that the *bands of law* could never evoke.

Nothing is more precious to a believer than the assurance: "Tenderly He watches over you, / Every step, every mile of the way." The vital question is *how?* It is not as an absolute Ruler who arbitrarily determines everything that shall happen. Instead, it is the tender care of a loving Father who is committed to our eternal well-being.

PART IV

Don't Fence Him In!

Dear Father:

Thank You for helping us to understand our hurting a little more. How grateful we are that You loved and trusted us enough to make us real persons with true freedom. It is hard to comprehend, but we are beginning to see that the only way this could happen was for You to limit yourself. We can only imagine how difficult that was for You. It does help us to know that You hurt, even weep, with us. We also thank You that miracles do happen. We have seen them! We confess that we do not understand why they do or do not occur. May we not seek to limit You to our human understanding. Help us to trust Your mysterious ways. For Jesus' sake.   *Amen.*

When we conclude that God has limited himself to the laws of His world, that still leaves us with a perplexing problem. At times God does break those laws! What about the exceptions? They are what we know as miracles, and they *do* happen. But this whole subject opens the door to many questions, with almost as many different answers. What are miracles? What makes them happen? Are miracles available "on call," or as the result of certain requirements? Can we tie them to need or worthiness?

There is so much that we don't understand about miracles. Unfortunately, many have made an exception a potential rule. Try as we might, we can't discover any rhyme or reason for their presence or absence. When all is said and done, the secret lies with God alone.

Yet we need to honestly face the questions that arise and refuse to accept any easy answers. Superficial solutions are about as supportive as cardboard bricks that give an attractive appearance but only a flimsy foundation. Sadly, many have built their faith on prefabricated miracles and have suffered the tragic collapse that inevitably follows.

Our concern is to relate miracles to what God has *promised* to do for us when we hurt. It could be that this is an area that God has *purposely* reserved for himself, where we are "off limits," because He refuses to be fenced in.

27

Miracles Do Happen!

Henry let out a scream and nearly fainted. Without realizing it, he had bumped the stick on the switch of the bandsaw. With a whir the saw roared into action, the wheels turning with blinding speed. It was the last hour of my last day on the job in the shipyard mold loft. My final task was to clean the sawdust out of the bandsaw. Carelessly, I had not turned off the switch or removed the extension stick that simplified its use. But there was no one within 25 yards of me, I thought. On my hands and knees I was brushing the sawdust out from the spokes of the wheel, *with my hand and arm through the spokes.* Unseen by me, Henry had approached from my blind side to say a final good-bye. Accidently he had touched the stick that snapped on the saw.

I never have, nor will I ever, understand what happened! A split second before the motor whirred on, "something" (or Someone!) said to me: "Take out your hand." I had not seen or heard anyone. I immediately yanked my hand, and the flashing spokes grazed my fingertips. Without that flash warning I would have undoubtedly lost my right hand and very likely part of my arm. Can you imagine what I think today when I see an empty right sleeve and then look at my good right hand and arm?

Yes, miracles of many kinds *do* happen. The verification of them is beyond any reasonable question. Many times they are miracles of physical healing. I have been privileged to witness several across more than 35 years of ministry as a pastor, teacher, and evangelist. Some of them have been in my own family. There has been indisputable professional certification. They include various malignant tumors (even an acute brain tumor), cancerous rectal polyps, a perforated colon (that *should* have caused death), etc. Their validity is beyond any reasonable doubt. As I was writing this very chapter, a pastor friend told me about his doctor, who had just witnessed a "medically impossible" miracle in one of his patients. The verified testimonials are endless.

There are miracles of many kinds. Every issue of the popular *Guideposts* magazine relates vivid accounts of God's miraculous action in times of accident, ill health, emergencies, unemployment, etc. Can any unbiased person deny the fact of miracles today?

In the light of what we concluded in the last section, these miracles represent a decisive divine intervention in the *normal* order of events. In these cases God is obviously *not* limited to the laws that govern our world. In fact, that is one of the basic definitions of miracle—"An event or action that apparently contradicts known scientific laws."[1] We have suggested that, in the usual course of events, God limits himself to the observance of the laws of His world. But without question, He makes exceptions! He does interfere with, or even interrupt, the natural order of things.

Let's examine this a little further.

28

An Exception
Not the Rule

I have never forgotten the look on her face, although it has been over 25 years. In total despair she asked: "Pastor, what is wrong with my faith?" Sister Green was a minister's widow about 90 years of age. Glaucoma, in its advanced stages, was stealing her eyesight. Her daughter, with whom she lived, had secured the finest of medical attention. But Sister Green would not accept the pessimistic prognosis of the doctors. Instead, she turned to a national TV "healer," who, by direct promise or at least strong implication, assured her that God would heal her blindness, *if she had enough faith.* But it had not happened. Now she could only conclude that her faith was somehow lacking. So, instead of her sunset years holding peace and contentment, after a lifetime of Christian service, she was living in doubt and despair.

Only God knows how often this same story can be told. It is in the area of divine healing that so many make the same mistake. They consider God's gracious exceptions the common rule of practice. Because God *does* miraculously heal *on occasion,* it is assumed that if conditions are right, He will heal anyone at any time.

We *could* explore biblical and theological arguments that clearly disprove the audacious claims of those who offer healing on a wholesale basis. But all we need to do is *honestly* face the facts of human experience *that we all know.* It is a fact, beyond any question, that not everyone who prays and even believes, is healed. The answer is given, even as Sister Green was told, that when healing does not come, it is due to a lack of faith. But that is no explanation. It is circular reasoning or argument after the fact. The erroneous basic premise is never examined; namely, that it is God's will to heal everyone. A wrong first premise can only result in a wrong conclusion.

Is not a big part of the problem found in the careless use of the whole idea of miracles? A miracle is not simply something wonderful, exciting, unusual, or extraordinary. Instead, it is that for which *there is no human explanation.* If you can explain it, then it isn't a miracle! Thus, by its very nature, a miracle is not an everyday occurrence. When miracles become commonplace, they cease being miracles. By definition a miracle is the result of divine intervention. We can't manipulate, let alone manufacture, such intervention.

So, when miracles *do* happen, we should see them for what they are, exceptions and not the rule. As an act of sovereign grace, God sees fit to *break into* the normal order of events. As suggested, it many times is an act of *physical* healing. But there are other forms of healing that are no less miraculous. Perhaps God breaks a miserable habit that has plagued us, or transforms a painful personality trait. Miracles have many other forms besides healing. It could be an *escape* from some potential tragedy, or *protection* from an unseen danger. At other times it might be *provision* for a distressing need. But in *every case* the miracle is an exception. It does not *always* happen! In fact, it does not happen commonly. Miracles are almost always unexpected.

It is often suggested by ministers, quite commonly on TV and radio, that miracles *can* happen every day in our lives, if we have enough faith. This not only reveals a total misunderstanding of the true nature of miracles, but also has many other tragic consequences. It is cruel, and even criminal, to promise miracles to the hopeless and despairing, as if they were for *anyone at any time.* God alone knows how many lives have been irreparably damaged and even destroyed by such fallacious offers. Instead of being encouraged to exercise faith in God's gracious promises (cf. Chap. 23), many have been led on a futile search for a miraculous deliverance. The result is that the faith of multitudes has been shattered, and uncounted numbers have ended up in cynicism, agnosticism, and even death.[1]

It is only Christian to *hope* that the proponents of perpetual miracles are *sincerely* confused. Perhaps some are carried beyond the limits of a defensible ministry because of their compassion for the sick and suffering. However, one wonders how many are similar to those with whom the apostles had to deal. Peter warned the saints that *many* would be involved with those who "shall ... make merchandise of you" (2 Pet. 2:3, KJV); and Paul castigated those who were literally "peddling" the Word of God (2 Cor. 2:17). Unfortunately, it would appear that there are many today who *peddle miracles.* All too often this is done for personal gain, as the estates they leave behind eloquently testify. We can only say with Paul, when dealing with such distressing situations, "Their condemnation is just" (Rom. 3:8).

God does, on occasion, intervene in the affairs of men. It is a serious mistake to make these gracious exceptions by God the rule for everyone.

29

No Rhyme nor Reason

Wini, my wife, was the first to notice and said to me: "Dick, can you see a change in Mary's face?" She had had a brain tumor in its advanced stages, and the left side of her face had been visibly drawn. Only a few weeks before she had undergone another in a series of painful brain surgeries. But this time the doctors were unable to even remove a portion of the inoperable tumor. They closed the incision, convinced that she had only a few months to live. We had access to all the medical information. Ruth, a church member, was the head of nursing service in the hospital and kept me fully informed. Indeed, there was no human hope.

Our youth group had a party for Mary's 16th birthday— six months early. She was so weak that most of her time was spent in bed. Yet she made the surprising announcement that she was going to attend the morning service of our soon-coming special youth meeting. It took a lot of doing, but on that Sunday morning Mary was there with her mother and sister. At the close of the service, when several came forward to pray, I was surprised to see Mary among them. To my knowledge no special prayer was made for her healing.

Now a few weeks had passed and, to our happy surprise, Mary had been present in every Sunday morning service. Having a view of the congregation from the piano bench, Wini had noticed the change in Mary's face. The drawn look was gone! When my attention was called to it, I also saw the change. Then I asked Ruth, our nurse friend, to take special notice, and she agreed with our conclusion. With some urging, Mary went back to the hospital for an examination. Then came the startling and unbelievable news that the tumor was gone! Mary finished high school, was married, and had several children. She is still in good health, the last I knew. Sadly, within six months of her healing, Mary left the church and never returned, and that was over 25 years ago. As far as I know, she never became active in church again.

The story of Mary's miraculous healing has been related for a special purpose. This is the most dramatic example of divine healing that I have ever witnessed, especially with the unusual medical confirmation. Yet there is no apparent reason why it should have happened, particularly when I remember the many for whom healing did not come. Mary's *need* was not exceptional compared with others I have ministered to. When we realize the shocking spiritual ingratitude that followed the miracle, there can be no question of a special worthiness. Without doubt this is the most difficult thing to understand about God's miraculous interventions. Not only are miracles unexpected and the exception rather than the rule, but there seems to be no rhyme nor reason to their appearance.

There doesn't appear to be, at least to our limited understanding, any rationale of *need* in connection with the presence or absence of miracles. It is not a matter of them coming for those who need them the most. Looking back over almost 25 years of pastoral ministry, I can remember repeated instances of my parishioners being in extreme, even desperate, need. Many times it would be for physical healing, but often for some other problem. I earnestly prayed for them; in private, in church, in their homes. But no miracles happened. Yet often at the same time, there were others whose need did not appear to be anywhere near as acute. Consequently, my pastoral concern was not as intense for them. Still, to my surprise, many times miraculous assistance came to them.

Often the element of need is not that of the person himself, but of his family, church, community, and even his country. We have all seen someone, whose presence was direly needed, who was suddenly taken. At the same time a person, with no particular responsibilities, was miraculously spared.

Of one thing we can be certain: God's miraculous activity is not related to our being worthy of it! In fact, I have almost been driven to the opposite conclusion. Even now, when I think of some of the saints with whom I spent hours in pastoral care, my heart *still* bleeds. Many of them are in heaven today, but only after months and even years of intense suffering. Then when I think of others who did experience a miraculous touch from God and remember how they had lived, I am baffled. Sometimes, even like Mary, it happened to them personally. At other times I have seen miracles in children's lives, whose parents were extremely ungrateful. Jim's small son Bobby was healed of malignant growths in his rectum. It was but a few months later that Jim, in a rage and still rebellious against God, threw Bobby more than 25 feet across the lawn. Many times in my churches there have been men who devotedly loved God and their family, but never seemed to be able to get their heads above water financially. At the same time some worldling, who had no thought of God and tragically neglected his family, seemed to find the key to instant prosperity. It doesn't *look* fair!

This is not easy to write about, but it is an all too well known fact of life. Many of us think about it, and we need the honesty to drag it out into the open and face it. God's special favors, if we want to call them that, are not dispensed on the basis of merit or worth.

I have learned that just as it is futile to look at adversity and insist on an answer to: "What did I do to deserve that?" so it is also fruitless to look at another's good fortune and ask: "What did he do to deserve that more than I?" The simple fact is that life here in this world is not set up with a balance sheet of merit and demerit. We believe that a day is coming when the books will be balanced. But that time is not now!

We must ever remember that God's miraculous interventions are acts of sovereign grace. They are not based on need or merit, at least as we can understand them. Instead, God acts for reasons known only to Him. It is to that we now turn.

30

Known Only to Him

"Prof, I *do trust* God, but you know about my mother!"
Yes, indeed I did know about Bob's mother. That morning in
the camp meeting service I had spoken on the parable of the
tares and the wheat. The message ended with a challenging
assertion that God was in control and "the devil can't hurt
us." Bob, singing in the college quartet, lived with a heartache that many could not bear. While he was still young, his
mother, a vivacious and musically talented pastor's wife, had
been stricken and left paralyzed. Now he was in college and
his mother was still helpless. That's a heavy burden to carry!

This is the *heart* of our problem. If it is true, as we have
concluded, that God doesn't arbitrarily control everything
that comes into our lives, but does on occasion intervene,
then *why* does He not do so in a tragic case like this? If God
can and *does* at times miraculously assist those in dire need,
why doesn't He help Bob's mother? Why did May, a member
of the college class I sponsored, unexpectedly die on the
operating table just before she was to graduate and begin a
life of fruitful ministry? If God *could* stop it, why didn't He?
Why did the infant daughter of Jean, my former secretary,
die from a crib death? God *knew* the years Jean and Jack had

waited to have a child, because they put Him first in their lives.

Such tragic stories are endless. There is simply no satisfactory answer, at least that I know of. Yes, we can project some ideas of why God doesn't intervene when *we think* He ought to. It is possible that God does not want to be put in the box of our understanding. He is still God Almighty and need not conform to the limits of our little minds. Several years ago Aunt Jane, one of the wisest Christians I have ever known, shared with me a gem of spiritual wisdom. She said: "It always troubles me when someone says that *they know for certain* what God will or will not do." As I pondered her observation, it became clear how right it was. When we are *certain* about what God will or should do, it is *our understanding* we are certain of. This is very dangerous because we are saying that *we* can't be wrong. It should never be forgotten that man is finite and ever prone to error, which includes our understanding.

Sometimes I wonder if at times God's miraculous interventions happen in order to make His promise come true. He has *guaranteed* that He would not *permit* anything to come into our lives that we could not handle by His grace (cf. 1 Cor. 10:13). But it is very possible that at times the only way victory can come is for God to miraculously intervene. He will move heaven and earth to keep us from being overwhelmed.

But when all is said and done, we still do not have a *rationally* satisfying answer as to why God does or does not miraculously intervene in our lives. We will never fully understand this side of heaven. This is the area of God's mysterious will. God *does* "move in a mysterious way / His wonders to perform." We must recognize and accept it as such. There have always been those who were certain they fully understood God's actions. Others have concluded that because *they* can't see an answer, there must not be one and God must be at fault. In a graduate seminar on Immanuel Kant, being conducted by a famous philosopher, a fledgling student made a dramatic pronouncement to his instructor in front of the whole group. "I have decided that anything I can't understand about God I refuse to believe." He expected a compliment, but the wise professor never said a word. Instead, he gave the young man the most eloquent look of pity I have ever seen. It doesn't take a lot of brilliance to see that *if* we understood everything about God, *He would be smaller than our minds.* I want a God who is bigger than I am!

The fact is that God acts in ways that are known *only* to Him. In my more lucid moments I know this is the way it *ought* to be and actually *must* be. Yet that does not seem to be so plain when my heart is hurting and it seems like God should do something. The knowledge of what *ought* and *must* be God's prerogatives doesn't help me much then.

That is why this is one of the most critical areas of faith, in the sense of trust. *I know that God loves me!* He demonstrated that love conclusively when He was willing to not even spare His own Son, when that was the *only* way to save my poor, lost soul. Can I not *trust* such a God as this? Should I not *rest* in His love when knowledge and understanding fail to bring me answers? Yes! I *should* and *must* trust Him and the certainty of His love. Then my faith is in God himself, and not in what I believe He is able or even going *to do.* I trust *Him,* even if there is no miracle, because I am confident of His love. This alone will bring peace to my troubled heart.

On the surface this might appear the same as trusting God's designs when adversity comes (cf. Chap. 16). But there is a crucial difference! It is one thing to have faith in God, when we believe He plans or specifically permits a

126

bitter tragedy. It is an entirely different thing to recognize that sometimes God miraculously intervenes on our behalf, for reasons known only to Him. When He doesn't act, it isn't because He approves what is happening. Thus, there is no question of why He has allowed the hurt that we are suffering. Instead, although we do not understand God's mysterious workings, we have faith in His love and our heart is at rest.

God's mysterious ways are known only to Him. In our final section we will briefly consider some of the practical implications of our faith in Him. To this we now turn.

PART V

What Do I Do Now?

Dear Father:

We are learning—thank You! How easy it is to increase our hurting by misunderstanding You. But we are seeing more clearly that You do not cause our troubles, either by plan or specific permission. You love us so much that most of all You want us to be real persons, so we can truly love You in return. We can see how this has caused You to make a very painful decision. The only way for us to be free is for You to limit yourself. But how grateful we are that You do, at times, intervene in our lives. We don't understand Your reasons for doing so, but we love You enough to trust You. So now help us to learn what You want us to do. Lord, teach us. We are listening. In Christ's name.   *Amen.*

Quite naturally, if what we have been saying is true, the question comes: "What is the use of praying?" Specifically, should we pray for miracles? This strikes at the heart of the meaning of prayer as petition and raises several vital questions.

Does our praying change the mind of God? Do we, in prayer, convince God to do something He has not wanted or planned to do? Is God waiting for us to demonstrate persistence in prayer before He will give an answer? What kind of faith does God expect us to have? How is faith related to praying: "Thy will be done"? Why should we pray for a miracle, if we do? What should we desire most when we pray?

These are difficult questions to answer! Yet we need to try to answer them if we are going to find the help God has for us. Lovingly He stands beside us, even in the darkest and most difficult hours, waiting to minister. It is *so* important that we not miss His grace and strength because of mistaken ideas or even prejudices. May we, with open and honest hearts, have the courage and faith to ask Him: "What do I do now?"

31

Should I Pray for Miracles?

It was late at night when Dr. Greenwich approached Brother and Sister James and me. He had just come from the operating room where they were doing emergency exploratory surgery on eight-year-old Jimmie James. The doctor's face was grave when he said: "We found the trouble; his large intestine is badly bruised. The only hope is to telescope the colon, but it is a very delicate operation. I am sorry that I can't promise you anything." I hurried to the phone and called my wife. Within a half hour a dozen or more gathered at the church altar. Long into the night we earnestly prayed for Jimmie's recovery.

In light of all we have been examining, should we pray for miracles? If God acts by sovereign grace, not based on any need or merit we can understand, then why pray? This is a very understandable question. As long as I can remember, when Wini and I begin a special trip, she always, within the first five minutes, prays for God's protection on the highway. The prayer for "traveling mercies" is almost automatic among those who love and serve God. We don't usually stop to think about it, but we really are asking God to *keep* anything from happening to us. Actually, it is a request for divine intervention, or a miracle, if it is necessary. Because it does not normally become necessary, we spend little time thinking about it until some tragedy occurs.

Should we pray for miracles? Of course we should! God knows the concerns of our hearts and *encourages* us to express them to Him. That is a vital part of our relationship together. But there are some things that we should remember. Always, as in any prayer, including one for a miracle, it *must be* conditioned by the request: "Thy will be done." How sad that some extremists refer to this as the "doubter's prayer"! They understand these wonderful words as indicating a lack of faith. If Jesus had to qualify His prayer in Gethsemane by those words, should we hesitate to pray the same way? "Thy will be done" can be voiced in many ways. It can depict despair, resignation, or bitterness. But it can also indicate a loving acceptance of and reliance upon God's love. We *should* not want anything but what is His will. God knows so much better than we do what is best.

How does our praying relate to miracles? Does our prayer make them happen? Of one thing we can be reasonably sure. *When we pray, we do not change the mind of God* in the sense of convincing Him to do something He has not wanted to do. Our prayer does not talk God into taking action! I know that my loving Father is *always* doing *all* for me that He is given opportunity to do. Yet, there is a mystery here that no one fully understands. Why pray? It is because *some things happen when we pray that would not have happened if we had not prayed.* Jimmie had a remarkable recovery following that midnight prayer meeting. Would it have happened if we had not prayed? No one can be certain, and it is possible that it could have happened without our prayers. But I know two parents and a pastor who have always believed that it wouldn't have happened! Explain it?

132

I can't, nor can anyone else. I wonder how much our praying gives God an *opportunity* He would not otherwise have. Beyond that we are not able to go.

Another idea is that miracles take place only when we *persist* in prayer. This is seen as a demonstration to God that we really mean business and are in earnest. So, *importunate prayer* is encouraged. This is an agonizing insistence, and even demand, that our prayer be answered. This can only mean that God is hesitant to answer our prayer until He is convinced that we genuinely mean it. Jesus' parables on importunity are usually quoted to support this concept.[1] But many New Testament scholars are convinced these are *parables of contrast* and depict how we *should not* pray to our Heavenly Father. I have a hard time seeing God as a "Reluctant Benefactor."

Quite often the necessary ingredient in the "formula" that produces miracles is identified as *faith added to our prayers.* If we have enough faith, miracles will happen. But what do we mean by "having enough faith"? One Sunday morning Sister Jones asked me to call on her as soon as possible. She was the unquestioned spiritual leader of our small church, as well as our pianist, treasurer, missionary president, a Sunday School teacher, etc. I wasn't prepared for what happened. "Pastor, after your sermon on faith Sunday morning, I had to talk to you." She was a retired schoolteacher and a "spiritual giant," while I was a fledgling pastor, not long out of school. She told me of a prayer meeting, several years earlier, when she and some of the other church folk gathered at the bedside of a dying saint. As they prayed, the heavens opened and God remarkably revealed himself to them. They all went home rejoicing, certain that Sister Mercer was healed. To everyone's shock, instead of being healed, she died before morning.

By now Sister Jones' eyes were filled with tears. "You

are the first one I have ever shared this with, but from that day to this I have never been able to have faith in God. The devil haunts me with doubt because of that incident." Following an emergency call for help (to God!), I tried to minister to her.

First, I repreached much of my Sunday sermon. It had been on the "Three Hebrew Children," who were thrown into the fiery furnace. When they told the king their God was able to deliver them, that was faith in the *ability* of God. Going on, they assured the king their God would deliver them, which is faith in the *activity* of God. Finally, they said that if their God didn't deliver them, they still would not bow down to the king's idol. This "but if not" is the highest level of faith, *faith in God himself, regardless.*

I explained that when our faith goes no higher than the activity of God, what we are certain God is going to do, it is actually *faith in our understanding.* Then I suggested that very possibly the amazing sense of God's presence was His gracious preparation for Sister Mercer's homegoing. But she, and the others, had *misunderstood* this and thought it was assurance that she would be healed. The fountain of tears broke and, after a few moments, Sister Jones smilingly confessed, "For the first time in several years, I have peace."

Some have pictured faith as almost mechanical and automatic, calling it "achieving faith." It has been even likened to a wavelength, or wire, such as a telephone line. When a "connection" is made, the answer is a certainty. However, when the connection is broken, an answer is impossible. Incredibly, some advocates of this theory have accepted the logical conclusion that a sinner's prayer would *have to be answered* if he had this kind of faith. In the most literal sense "believing makes it so!"

Unfortunately, there is a widespread misunderstanding about the miracles of Jesus. It has been commonly assumed

134

that they are always accompanied by faith. I have several times led a graduate seminar, studying the miracles of Jesus, and we always have come to the same conclusion: *On the basis of the biblical record, there is no consistent relationship between faith and miracles in the ministry of Jesus.* Sometimes the individual (in need) has faith and sometimes not, other times another person (than the needy person) has faith, and many times there is no mention of faith. So it is totally invalid to insist that faith was necessary for miracles in the ministry of Jesus.

What can we conclude? *Sometimes miracles do happen when we pray.* But the suggestion which some make, that you can have your own miracle every day, is totally unwarranted. As suggested earlier (cf. Chap. 28), such a concept denies the basic nature of miracles. Undoubtedly we all need more faith and could profitably search our hearts at this point. However, to make faith a mechanical or automatic means of obtaining miracles is invalid almost to the point of absurdity.

Should we pray for a miracle? A big part of the answer relates to *why* we want one. Mike is a warm friend of mine, and we spend many hours together every summer in Maine. After a lifetime of disillusionment and indifference to God and the church, he was remarkably converted when he was about 60 years of age. His conversion was brought about by the miraculous healing of a grandchild. Today he is firmly convinced that more miracles are needed to spread the gospel. Of course, we are all partial to the factors that have influenced us. Perhaps we should pray for miracles with this end in view. Yet, in the story of the rich man and Lazarus there is a vital word of caution (Luke 16:19-31). Abraham told Dives that even if God sent someone back from the dead (could there be a more startling miracle?), his brothers would still not change. His brothers had the Scriptures (the

Law and the Prophets) and needed nothing more. It is highly questionable how many would be *meaningfully* influenced by miracles today.

Certainly we should not pray *selfishly* for a miracle. I have been shocked, as a pastor, at the times when that in fact was the case. Should I pray for a miracle so that it may be better *for me?* Jesus, with all His supernatural powers, *never performed a miracle for His own benefit!* It was this specific temptation of Satan that He resisted in the wilderness. Every miracle of Jesus was *to help others.* This should guide us in our concern for miracles.

32

Lord, Keep Me Close!

At least a dozen times I started the letter I knew I had to write. In Chapter 2 I mentioned how Jim, a student of mine, had suddenly been stricken with leukemia. Now I had to write to him. What could I say? Words on paper are so cold! Then a thought came to me, which I believe was inspired.

I wrote how Paul had struggled with the greatest problem of his life in Romans 9—11. If all he had said (Romans 1—8) was true, then Israel was lost! He couldn't reconcile this with them being God's chosen people. How could it possibly work out right? He tried one *rational* answer after another—the total sovereignty of God (Chap. 9), the responsible freedom of man (Chap. 10) and the ultimate purpose of God (the allegory of the olive tree, Chap. 11). But in none of these could Paul find peace of mind. So, finally he cried: "Oh, the depth of the riches both of the wisdom and knowledge of God! How unsearchable are His judgments and unfathomable His ways!" (Rom. 11:33). Here he found peace, resting by faith in the mysterious ways of God.

I tried to tell Jim that no one could give him a rational answer to the tragedy that was closing the curtain of his life. If he insisted on searching for such, it would only bring further despair and pain. But, like Paul, he could find peace as he trusted a loving God. This is faith and not fatalism! It is faith, as defined in the last chapter, *in God himself— regardless.*

Jim's condition stabilized, as the malignancy temporarily went into remission. He even was able to return to school for a semester. One of my most grateful, and humbling, memories is the day Jim stood at my desk and told me, "Prof, of all the many letters I received, God used yours to bring peace to my heart." Can you imagine what passed through my mind a few months later when I sat in Jim's memorial service?

When all is said and done, there is *no totally satisfying rational answer to the problem of suffering.* Peace of mind and heart are only found in the "eternal dimension" of faith in God—regardless. Asking "Why?" can only increase the pain and misery. The reason is clear. It is extremely difficult, if possible at all, to ask, "Why?" in a Christian manner. Almost inevitably, "Why?" is a question of defiance that is demanding a vindication rather than being a genuine request for information. We can only find peace as we ask, "What?" instead of "Why?" *"What" is there for me to learn and do in and through this experience?*

A strange thing has been happening lately, as I have faced adversity and the unknown, even when it involved my service for Him. Once it was while I lay in the intensive care ward, not knowing if my sudden attack was my heart or gall bladder. This was just a day or two before a new semester was to begin. Another time my flight was long overdue because of fog, and there seemed no human way to reach the opening service of a Bible conference, where I was to speak. Still another time I was afflicted with a severe cold only days before an exceptionally heavy preaching schedule. Such examples could be multiplied.

Once I would have pled for a miracle! After all, I needed it to serve Him. But now there was a great peace as I reminded Him that it was all known to Him. "If You want to intervene, Father, I will be grateful. But if not, it is all right. *Most of all, keep me close to You.*"

I am learning to find a new peace as I face the unknown. Every year in May, Wini and I start a trip of several thousand miles on the increasingly dangerous highways. No longer do I ask for God's "traveling mercies" (meaning special protection). Instead, my prayer is: "Lord, keep us so close to You that no matter what happens, we can find in Your presence all that we need." Some would deny that is faith and would say it is only fatalism. But I strongly disagree! It is faith in God—regardless!

But when the journey has ended and we have returned safely, should we give thanks to God? As I was preparing to write this very chapter, Bob, the pastor for whom I had just held a Bible conference, was driving me to the airport. We were visiting and he didn't see, as soon as he should have, the car in front of us suddenly stop. So he had to quickly apply his brakes, and we skidded on the rain-swept highway into the opposite lane. If a car had been meeting us, we would have had a serious accident. Although the traffic was heavy, at that precise moment the other lane was empty. With a sigh of relief we both said: "Thank God!"

And we both meant it. Maybe God didn't have anything *specifically* to do with it. But a vital part of a Christian view of life is a *spirit* and *attitude* of gratitude. We were grateful and our gratitude was directed toward a loving God in whom "we live, and move, and have our being" (Acts 17:28, KJV). May I ever live close enough to Him that at any moment I will find Him by my side—"just when I need Him most."

We have tried to honestly face what is undoubtedly the most agonizing problem that man knows—the problem of suffering. There is no better way to close than with what I think are the greatest words that Bill and Gloria Gaither have ever written:

> In the garden He went to pray when it seemed hope was gone.
> He prayed with a broken heart, and He prayed all alone.
>
> Have you had a Gethsemane? Have you prayed the night through?
> Have you shed tears of agony, when no hope was in view?
> Have you prayed, "If it be Thy will, may this cup pass from me?
> But if it's Thy will, dear Lord, I will bear it for Thee."
>
> Have you had a Gethsemane? Have you prayed the night through?
> In the dark of those dreary hours, did the Lord come to you?*

Notes

Preface

1. Joni Eareckson and Steve Estes, *A Step Further* (Grand Rapids: Zondervan Publishing House, 1978), p. 14.

2. Cf. *The Christian's Secret of a Happy Life.*

Introduction

1. Eric Marshall & Stuart Hample, comp., *More Children's Letters to God* (New York: Simon & Schuster, 1967).

2. *Newsweek,* May 9, 1977, p. 15.

Chapter 4

1. Marjorie Lewis' *The Hurting Parent* is strongly recommended.

Chapter 7

1. Henry David Thoreau, *Walden.*

Chapter 10

1. A paraphrase of Thomas Hardy's famous quote: "'Justice' was done, and the President of the Immortals ... had ended his sport with Tess." Thomas Hardy, *Tess of the D'Urbervilles* (New York: Harper & Brothers, 1920), p. 457.

Chapter 16

1. "Be anxious for nothing, but in everything by prayer and supplication with thanksgiving let your requests be made known to God. And the peace of God, which surpasses all comprehension, shall guard [garrison] your hearts and your minds in Christ Jesus" (Phil. 4:6-7). "In everything give thanks; for this is God's will for you in Christ Jesus" (1 Thess. 5:18). "Always giving thanks for all things in the name of our Lord Jesus Christ to God, even the Father" (Eph. 5:20).

Chapter 19

1. This is seen in Matthew, the most Jewish Gospel account, where repeatedly it is said that an event happened *in order that* an Old Testament

prophecy might be fulfilled (cf. Matt. 4:14 et al.). It means no more than that *as a result* of the event the prophecy was fulfilled.

2. The devil also omitted the very important clause: "to guard you in all your ways" (Ps. 91:11).

Chapter 21

1. Cf. the chapter "The Shocking Alternative" (Book 2, chap. 3) in C. S. Lewis, *Mere Christianity* (New York: Macmillan Co., 1960).

2. Charles Colson, *Born Again* (Old Tappan, N.J.: Fleming H . Revell Co., Chosen Books, 1976), pp. 122-23.

Chapter 23

1. The Greek term, *peiradzō,* has the basic meaning of "to test," which in some restricted cases means "to tempt."

2. Some other translations read: "more than conquerors" (KJV, RSV, NIV), or "overwhelming victory" (NEB, Phillips).

Chapter 24

1. "If the Lord wills" (1 Cor. 4:19; Jas. 4:15), "if God wills" (Acts 18:21), if "the Lord" (God) permits (1 Cor. 16:7; Heb. 6:3), "if the will of God" (1 Pet. 3:17, marg.). Paul speaks of journeying "by the will of God" (Rom. 1:10; 15:32).

Chapter 26

1. Note the popularity of *The Living Bible,* prepared explicitly for children.

Chapter 27

1. *Webster's New World Dictionary.*

Chapter 28

1. As I was writing this chapter, I was told of a lady in Portland, Me., who had turned her back on medical treatment, claiming to be miraculously healed. She was dead in a matter of weeks.

Chapter 31

1. The "unrighteous judge" (Luke 18:1-8), and the "friend . . . at midnight" (11:5-13).